More Than Conquerors

More Than Conquerors

Steven Masood

**OM
publishing**

First published 2000 by OM publishing

OM Publishing is an imprint of Paternoster Publishing,
PO Box 300, Carlisle, Cumbria, CA3 0QS, UK
and
PO Box 1047, Waynesboro, GA 30830-2047, USA.

04 03 02 01 00 99   7 6 5 4 3 2 1

British Library Cataloguing in Publication Data
A catalogue record for this book is available from
the British Library.

ISBN 1-898938-83-0

Typeset by Reesprint, Radley, Oxfordshire, OX14 3AJ.

Printed and bound in Great Britain by
Caledonian International Book Manufacturing, Glasgow.

Contents

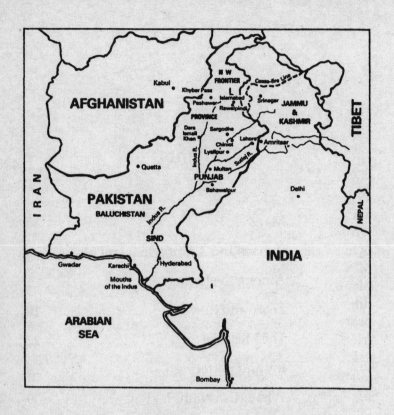

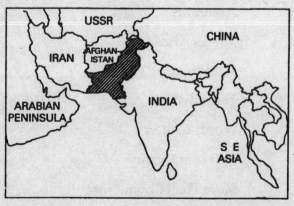

Preface and Acknowledgements

Since the publication of *Into the Light* (OM/Paternoster 1986,87,92,97) friends have asked me, 'What happened after you became a Christian?' Others have asked me to write a sequel. My reply is that I was rejected by my own family and the Muslim community but various Muslim and Christian friends, groups and agencies played a great part in my life to comfort me in my dilemmas. I have refrained from writing a sequel in order to safeguard the various ministries of these friends.

However, I am able to share in this book, *More Than Conquerors*, some highlights of the happenings of the first few years after my conversion. The following pages are a window into the occasions when I shared the Gospel with fellow Muslims. The story revolves around my survival as a Christian, the sudden death of one of my dearest friends and the memories of the discussions that took place between us.

The author gratefully acknowledges the contribution of the Drummond Tract Society to this publication.

All Qur'anic references are taken from:

1. Muhamad Marmaduke Pickthal, *The Meaning of The Glorious Qur'an* (Karachi: Taj Company, n.d.)

2. Abdullah, Yusuf Ali, *The Holy Qur'an: Text, Translation and Commentary* (Maryland: Amana Corp., 1983).

1

Among the Living

Atif was my best friend. Many of our acquaintances thought we were brothers or close relatives. But now, he was no longer among the living. He was involved in a fatal accident. He was run over by a truck. He was taken to hospital but died on the way. The city of Karachi where we both lived has a bad record of road deaths but I had never thought that one day my friend would also join its number. At his funeral, friends, relatives and neighbours paid their respects and offered condolences to the family. After the funeral prayer, his body was buried in the graveyard with respect according to tradition and custom.

I glanced around and there were rows and rows of graves, some very old and some new. I thought about the people who were buried there, young and old, even small children. We come into this world, live for a while and then death claims us. Not only bad but also good people die. Both Muslims and Christians believe that there is a day coming when all the dead will be raised to face judgement.

'Would I see Atif again on that day?' I asked myself. Like anybody else I washed my hands at the water pump near the gate of the grave yard and followed the others out of the grounds.

Although I was walking among the living and was in the midst of hustle and bustle, my attention was elsewhere. The scene of Atif's burial kept repeating itself in my mind. Just half an hour ago I saw his face and now I would never see him again on this earth. I thought about the Muslim belief that when people have buried their dead and left the graveyard, when they are about forty paces from the grave, two angels, Munkar and Nakir, interrogate the dead man in the grave. They ask three questions: 'Who is your God? Who is your Prophet? What is your religion?'

I stood at the bus stop waiting for a bus which seemed never to come. On the horizon I could see the sun like a red circle disappearing behind some buildings. Atif and I liked watching the sunset and the different colours that followed it in the sky. Some Muslims do not like the sunset, they think it represents decline, death and the victory of darkness. Atif used to argue with such friends saying, 'Yes, but it also reminds us that there is hope for tomorrow. There will be a sunrise and then its light will overcome all the darkness.'

I remembered the first time I went with Atif to see the sunset. When the sun disappeared from our sight, we could only see red, purple and grey streaks on the horizon. I heard Atif reciting a eulogy followed by the first chapter of the Qur'an while looking in the direction of the sun going down:

Oh Allah! You are free from all defects. I praise you. Blessed is your name. Exalted is your majesty and sublime is your praise. There is none worthy of worship except you... In the name of Allah, the Beneficent, the Merciful. Praise be to Allah, Lord of the Worlds. The Beneficent, the Merciful. Owner of the Day of Judgement. Thee (alone) we worship; Thee (alone) we ask for help. Show us the straight path, the path of those whom Thou hast favoured; Not (the path) of those who earn Thine anger nor of those who go astray.

For me it was nothing new. Muslims start the day by reciting it in their morning prayers and end the day by reciting it in the late evening prayers. Their 'Good morning' starts with it and 'Good night' is sealed by reciting it. In fact it is recited in all five daily obligatory prayer sessions. Muslims recite it at the beginning of their work; they repeat it before or after the signing of contracts and documents. They recite it as they welcome loved ones and as they bid them farewell. They recite it as they welcome the news of a birth and they repeat it at the end of a life.

Somebody pushed me and I realised that the bus had arrived. All the way home my mind was still muddled with memories of the things that Atif and I had shared, the conversations, the arguments and our affection for each other. At home that night I could not sleep. Everything was the same yet seemed different. After long hours of tossing and turning, at last I went to sleep.

When I woke up the next morning, the need to be at the sorting office on time overrode everything else. I didn't want to go but I still made myself leave for work. If I lost my job, how would I survive? Where would I live? Where would my next meal come from? I was already having a bad time in the office. Some of my colleagues were unhappy with me because I did not want to join their 'games' of stealing and laundering. Being a convert to the Christian faith, a few had accused me of apostasy and of being sympathetic to Christian missionary work by releasing mail and packages addressed to Christians without proper censorship. In spite of such accusations, I had so far survived in a job in the postal service.

At work that day, a few people mentioned Atif's unusual and sudden death and showed sadness, while the rest continued as if nothing had happened. I kept thinking about him and his good friendship. The last time, had it not been for his support and witness, I would have lost my job. On that occasion, one of my co-workers pinched a registered letter from the pile on my table. At the end of the working day it became obvious. I was about to be charged for theft. Then Atif remembered my co-worker removing a packet from my table, in an odd way, when I was not looking. The article was found, but though I was cleared of suspicion, the guilty party was never punished.

Unusually, it was a quiet day but then, just an hour before the end of my duty for the day my supervisor, who had never liked me because of my different religious beliefs, came to me with a charge sheet from the Superintendent accusing me of some negligence again. The same person who had some years ago himself filled in the form for me and had made sure I passed smoothly through the selection and training procedure was now threatening to sack me.

The situation prompted me to buy a newspaper and look for a job. That evening, sitting in a cheap corner café after a so-called evening meal, and sipping a cup of sugary tea which must have been boiled more than twenty times, I looked at all the columns of situations vacant, but to no avail. There was nothing I could apply for. I soon realised that I had been sitting there for such a long time that the shop assistant was feeling uneasy and was expecting me to order more food and drink or to leave. I had neither room nor inclination to ask for more of that dreadful sweet-tasting tea and so I folded the paper, tucked it under my arm and left.

To pass the time that evening, at home as usual, I tried to read. After a few pages, I did not remember anything. The previous sleepless nights got the better of me and I fell fast asleep, only to be woken early the next morning by the high-pitched clucking of the next-door neighbours' chickens. Such a commotion was not unusual. Whenever a cat attacked them, they made such a noise. I got up and looked through the window. A big healthy cat passed by on the front wall holding a young chicken in its mouth. What a breakfast for a cat to start the day with!

I was glad there was still sufficient water in the tank for me to wash and get ready. After a cup of tea and a piece of bread I was about to leave when I realised it was my day off. The thought of a break made me feel especially happy. On such a day I would often go to Atif's home or he would come over and we would both spend the day together at the seashore or in a park or somewhere else. Today, however, there was no one to come and knock on the door and shout, 'Come on, let's get out of here.'

I just could not bear to sit at home all day, and felt that I had to go somewhere, anywhere, before going to Atif's home that afternoon to take part in the funeral rites known as *So'yam*. I took the first bus that arrived at the stop. I was not sure where the bus was going and just asked the conductor to give me a ticket for wherever the local bus terminated.

Looking out of the window, I could see that everything was the same, the same noise of people and car engines. The same view of side-road vendors occupying the footpath, pushing pedestrians off the kerb to walk on the road and be hit by oncoming vehicles. I saw the signboards for Jinnah Park and Frere Hall. Then there was the library where Atif and I used to go and study; to read newspapers and magazines. In the park nearby, under the shade of the trees we used to sit for hours and argue about social and religious issues.

Like many religious people, he was a great believer in the day of judgement. To end an argument he would give up and say, 'Well, the day is coming when all will be revealed', and I would respond, 'By then it may be too late to repent' and we would both laugh. Although our religious feelings and ideologies were different, it had not affected our friendship.

'The bus terminates here.' The conductor's voice boomed in my ear and I got to my feet. It took me some time to struggle off the bus as a big crowd was trying to get on. Somehow I successfully reached the ground. The breeze from the sea was refreshing. I was at the pleasure beach at Clifton.

For a long time I sat on the promenade watching the rolling tide. There were children, young people even the elderly playing on the sand and in the water. A passing vendor persuaded me to buy some cola and a burger. Although I sipped the cola my appetite had vanished. When a *faqir* (beggar) asked me for some money, I offered him the freshly packed burger. He refused it saying that he was not hungry but needed some money. When I gave him some, he took the burger as well, and the next thing I knew, his dog was eating it and looking at me as though with grateful eyes.

A few yards away, I saw birds trying to take food from a child's hand. Further on, a group of men and women and their children were having a picnic. The old folk were sitting enjoying their drinks while the children under their watchful eyes were giggling, splashing and running after each other in the water.

I decided to take a stroll. I removed my shoes, rolled my trousers up to my knees and started walking on the wet sand. The sound of the waves, the cries of birds, the laughter and murmur of conversation all seemed somewhat soothing. I felt that before I was lonely and afraid, but now I felt part of the humanity around me. Although I had lost a good friend I was still among the living, and perhaps I could have other friends like Atif.

'Could I?' I asked myself.

Walking, watching, observing and most of the time deep in my thoughts, I realised I had come a long way and was approaching a fishing village. In the distance, I saw a police van with several people around it. Curiosity took me over to see what had happened. The body of a man in a smart suit lay there perforated with bullets. A policeman was searching his pockets but there was nothing to identify him.

'He must be a smuggler', somebody said. Another argued, 'Perhaps somebody killed him for his money.'

'No, no, his family or his son might have killed him to inherit his wealth', someone else remarked. There were many comments.

To disperse the growing crowd around the body,

another of the policemen waved his heavy stick, the infamous lathi: *'Chalo! Chalo! Tamasha nahi laga'* (Move along now. This is not a side show).

I walked away from the scene, thinking how many like him would be found dead today by police in the city, in the country, in the world. How many more would die today?

'Oh, but how many will be born today? Have you thought about that? The population is growing.' I asked myself.

'If a few disappear, it will not make a difference to those living. We are already facing a population explosion.' These remarks from a debate I had seen on television came back to me and I cried inwardly, 'How dare people talk in such a way on chat shows making it sound as if human life had no value at all.'

I turned around and started walking back in the direction of the promenade. There was a man standing in the water holding some strange beads and clay plates and cups. He was throwing bread into the water and I realised that he must have retired from a self-imposed time of confinement and solitude in which he hoped to gain some spiritual power of mystical communication. Whether he was successful or not, I, for one was glad that the food he was throwing in the water was a good meal for the birds, who were swooping on it with great enthusiasm.

Here were these birds which were not hired to work and be paid in order to eat and live. It reminded me of what Jesus said:

I tell you, do not worry about your life, what you will eat or drink; or about your body, what you will wear. Is not life more important than food, and the body more important than clothes? Look at the birds of the air; they do not sow or reap or store away in barns and yet your heavenly Father feeds them. Are you not much more valuable than they? Who of you by worrying can add a single hour to his life? (Matthew 6:25–27).

2

Peace and Reward

I looked at my watch. It was time to leave and take a bus to Atif's home. Although I had not been asked to attend the *So'yam*, the third-day funeral rites, I felt I should go and at least identify myself with the family's loss. Atif had one elder brother. His father had died when he was just a teenager. He was fortunate enough to have a mother who loved him dearly. She was in shock as she tried to take in the fact that her younger son was no longer with them.

Because it was the peak hour of the day, I was able to get on the bus comfortably. The driver was speeding. Another bus from another company using the same route was following us and he did not want his rival to get his custom. They were both overtaking each other and sometimes even racing in parallel. The passengers were not happy but the driver and his assistant paid no attention to their complaints. For me, the result was that I was an hour early and still safe and sound when I got off the bus.

Atif's front gate was ajar. The rites were about to begin. Like the others, I removed my shoes and entered the room where a big white cloth was laid, almost covering the floor of the whole sittingroom. All the chairs and other furniture had been shifted to make room for more people to come in and sit. I looked around and saw Hassan, Atif's brother, in a corner talking quietly with somebody. We embraced each other and he started crying like a child. Tears also came to my eyes. We both sat down, wiping our eyes.

In the course of this rite, friends and relatives usually read all 30 parts of the Qur'an so as to call down blessing and reward on the deceased. Some people hire professional reciters of the Qur'an for the purpose. However, here the obligation was carried out voluntarily by friends and family. After a while somebody passed me part of the Qur'an to recite, but Hassan quickly intervened and told him that I was not a suitable candidate. He thus gave it to someone sitting next to me. Several people by now were reciting the pages of the Qur'an. Hassan very soon excused himself to look into some matter in the house, and to occupy myself I started concentrating on what was taking place. Although a few were sitting quietly, others were reciting different parts of the Qur'an. The young teenage boy on my right was reciting the sixth part of the Qur'an. I could see over his shoulder what he was reciting:

Lo! We inspire thee as We inspired Noah and the prophets after him, as We inspired Abraham and Ishmael and Isaac and Jacob and the tribes, and Jesus and Job and Jonah and Aaron and Soloman, and as We imparted unto David the Psalms; And messengers We have mentioned unto thee before and messengers We have not mentioned unto thee; and Allah spake directly to Moses; Messengers of good cheer and of warning, in order that mankind might have no argument against

Allah after the messengers. Allah is ever Mighty, Wise
(Surah 4:163–165).

The young man turned the page and I stopped reading. But it brought back many memories of my search
for the truth. It was in the very pages of the Qur'an
where I had read, 'This is the Scripture whereof there is
no doubt, a guidance unto those who ward off (evil)'
(Surah 2:2). I remembered the way I used to interpret
this and argue with my teachers.

For me the Qur'an was a book in which there is guidance not for everybody, not for those who recite it idly,
in passing, or who repeat it without thinking, and
without bothering to research and study it to find the
precious jewels of guidance, but for those who act
piously.

Who are the pious? I used to argue that they were
those who not only observed the *Salah* (obligatory
prayers) and *zakah* (the giving of charity) but also
believed in what came before the Qur'an. I remembered the days when I began to find everything in the
Qur'an, and it was all new. I loved it, and its study
became my all-absorbing passion, which never ceased
to occupy my attention.

The Qur'an had captivated my waking hours. In
intense rapture I used to leaf through its pages, trying
to absorb its teachings. I remembered how the very
pages of the Qur'an referred me to the truth of the earlier scriptures, the Torah, the Zabur and the Injil.
Where were they? Where was I? What was this I was
starting to discover?

I really thank and praise God, who opened my eyes
and enlightened my understanding. I also thank

Muhammad, the Prophet of Islam, who claimed to have carried the message in the Qur'an. Here was I, weak, confused and wayward, who had asked for guidance more than 36 times a day in his ritual prayers saying, '*Ihadinah siratal Mustaqim*', (Show me the Straight Way), and God had given me a message through the pages of the Qur'an directing me to books which would lead me to that Straight Way.

I looked over the young man's shoulder to see what he was now reciting and saw written there in the Qur'an:

> How come they unto thee for judgement when they have the Torah, wherein Allah hath delivered judgement (for them)? ... Lo! We did reveal the Torah, wherein is guidance and a light, by which the Prophets who surrendered (unto Allah) judged the Jews, and the rabbis and the priests (judged) by such of Allah's scripture as they were bidden to observe, and there unto were they witnesses ... And We caused Jesus, son of Mary, to follow in their footsteps, confirming that which was (revealed) before him, and We bestowed on him the Gospel wherein is guidance and a light, confirming that was (revealed) before it in the Torah – a guidance and an admonition unto those who ward off (evil) (Surah 5:43,44,46).

'O, the boundless mercy of God!' I said quietly to myself. He looked at me in surprise. Perhaps my exclamation had been loud enough for him to hear. I apologised and he went back to his recitation. Still I could not stop my thinking and praising God for his knowledge.

In my search for the truth I found many passages in

the Qur'an which placed great value on the light and guidance to be found in the earlier scriptures. What a fitting description, for the lost and wayward, who grope in desperation and utter darkness for a light to lead them to their life's true goal. I remembered how my study of the Qur'an had persuaded me to get the Torah and the Gospel and to start studying them sincerely in order to understand the greatness of the One who revealed them.

After half an hour, all the readings from the Qur'an were finished. Hassan came in and asked me to follow him to another room where his mother wanted to meet me. Reluctantly I followed him. On seeing me, she quickly moved forward and embraced me.

'Masood! please do something. Help him to come back.' She was pleading.

'Ask Jesus to send him back.' She was weeping and crying. The ladies around her were surprised. Even Hassan had not expected this and was shocked.

To overcome the situation and keep Atif's affiliation with Christianity a secret, Hassan quickly said, 'O, Mum! Come on. We all have to go sooner or later. He will certainly rise on the Last Day. He is in a better place than this world.'

'I want to go after him.' She pleaded, 'Please let me go after him.'

It was difficult to control her. Hassan told me it would be better if we left and we went back to the room where the men were sitting.

The assistant Imam had arrived. Hassan greeted him. We all sat quietly. For a while there was a complete silence. One could have heard a pin drop. Then the Imam raised his hands in prayer and everyone followed. He prayed for the family, for forgiveness and reward for the deceased Atif and for patience and guidance for his brother and mother. After that Hassan distributed gifts among those who had partaken in the recitation of the Qur'an and later everyone was invited to share in a meal that the neighbours had prepared.

On the way back that evening, I kept thinking about Atif's mother. It reminded me of the Gospel story about a man named Lazarus who was raised from the dead by Jesus (John 11:1–44). I kept thinking that although Jesus raised him to life, he had to die again because the human body and the environment we live in dictate that our lives must eventually end. Only at Jesus' second coming will he raise his people to eternal life in fellowship with God and in his Kingdom.

Jesus made a firm promise: 'I will come again' (John 14:23). He said that his second coming would bring eternal life to those who believed in him and eternal destruction to those who rejected him (Matthew 24:30–31; 25:31–34). In another place he said, 'Behold, I am coming soon! My reward is with me, and I will give to everyone according to what he has done' (Revelation 22:12).

I thought about the perplexity on the faces of the ladies around Atif's mother who must have been wondering what her talk of Jesus meant. Did they sense some kind of affiliation? Atif had suffered some hard times just because he was my friend. Some colleagues at work had tried to persuade him not to associate with me, but he had refused to be dictated to and followed his own mind and reasoning.

Our friendship began during one of our training sessions at the Postal Services Institute. On one weekend trip he was my room-mate and one morning saw me reading the Bible. He was deeply concerned. He had been pleased that from being a member of the Ahmadiyya sect, I had come to accept Sunni Islam, but he was alarmed to see that now I had become a Christian.

'How can you believe a book which has been corrupted and changed?' he asked me adding, 'Christians have added their own words to their scripture.'

I was delighted that here was somebody who wanted to know why I believed in the reliability of the Torah and Injil. I could not keep silent. I felt compelled to share my joy with all my friends, and acquaintances who became dear to me. I shared with Atif how the Qur'an had been my constant companion and seized the opportunity to relate to him the discovery that had made me believe in the earlier Scriptures revealed to Moses, David and Jesus. I read to him from the Qur'an I had with me:

> He hath revealed unto thee (Muhammad) the Scripture with truth, confirming that which was (revealed) before it, even as He revealed the Torah and the Gospel.
>
> Aforetime, for a guidance to mankind; and hath revealed the Criterion (of right and wrong). Lo! those who disbelieve the revelations of God, there will be a heavy doom. Allah is Mighty, Able to Requite (the wrong) (Surah 3:3,4).

He quickly responded, 'But the Torah mentioned has been altered by the Jews, and the Gospel of Jesus has been tampered with by Christians.'

'Is it possible', I asked, 'that the Qur'an would declare the Torah to be guidance and light for people if it had been changed?'

I read another passage which plainly instructs the people of the Scriptures, Jews and Christians, 'Ye have naught (of guidance) till ye observe the Torah and the Gospel and that which was revealed unto you from your Lord.' (Surah 5:68).

I shared with Atif how I had studied, digging deep, researching, by myself and for myself, to find the answer to the queries like: Have the Scriptures been altered, corrupted or changed? Did the change take place before the Qur'an was revealed to Muhammad? If the change had taken place before the Qur'an, the Torah and Injil would not have been declared as guidance and light for people. The Qur'an would have declared them not as light but darkness; not as guidance for the faithful but as leading them astray.

If on the other hand it is said that the Jews and Christians changed the Torah and the Injil when they heard Muhammad's claims in the Qur'an then the Qur'anic revelation would also have mentioned this because it continued until Muhammad's death. How could it be changed when Allah himself ordered Muhammad to ask those who read the Torah and the Injil to confirm his faith in moments of doubt?

'And if thou (Muhammad) art in doubt concerning which we reveal unto thee, then question those who read the Scriptures (that were) before thee' (Surah 10:94).

Muhammad was told to ask those who possess the Reminder:

And we verily gave Moses and Aaron the Criterion (of right and wrong) and a light and a Reminder for those who keep from evil (Surah 21:48).

And We sent not (as Our messengers) before thee other than men whom We inspired. Ask the followers of the Reminder if ye know not (Surah 21:7).

The *Reminder* referred to here is the Jewish Scriptures and those who believe in it are called the followers of the Reminder or *Ahlez zikr (ahladh-dhekr)*. It is also impossible to substantiate the claim that the Torah and the Injil were altered after the revelation and compilation of the Qur'an. At the time of the Prophet of Islam the Torah and Injil had already been distributed throughout the civilised world and had even been translated into several languages.

Christianity, which had been established six hundred years before, had divided into contending factions. It would have been impossible to bring all the leaders of disagreeing churches to agree upon the changes to be made in the Torah or the Injil for good reasons or bad. And how could they have collected every copy of the books from different parts of the world?

Above all, is it possible that God, who knows the future and has known the end since the beginning, and from whom no secrets are hidden, would order us on one hand to stand fast by the Torah and the Injil while on the other hand allowing them to be changed? To believe in such a notion is to question God's foreknowledge and honour.

I was delighted that Atif knew the Qur'an and referred to passages which he believed were proof that the earlier scripture, known today as the Bible, has been altered. He took my copy of the Qur'an and read those passages to me:

> Can ye (O ye men of Faith) entertain the hope that they will believe in you? Seeing that a party of them heard the Word of God, and perverted it knowingly after they understood it (Surah 2:75).

> Of the Jews there are those who displace words from their (right) places, and say: We hear and we disobey (Surah 4:46).

> And because of their breaking the covenant, We have cursed them and made hard their hearts. They change words from their context and forget a part of that whereof they were admonished. Thou wilt not cease to discover treachery from all save a few of them. But bear with them and pardon them. Lo! God loveth the kindly (Surah 5:13).

> O Messenger! Let not them grieve thee who vie one with another in the race to disbelief, of such as say with their mouths: 'We believe,' but their hearts believe not, and of the Jews: listeners for the sake of falsehood on behalf of other folk who come not unto thee, changing words from their context and saying: If this be given unto you, receive it, but if this be not given unto you, then beware! (Surah 5:41).

Atif was very firm in his conclusion that these passages proved that changes had been made. He argued that I was misquoting and misinterpreting and asked me how I could account for these passages which stated that changes had been made in the earlier scriptures. We were joined by another student who was furious at my daring to use the Qur'an in my arguments.

I told him that I was sharing what I had found in the Qur'an to make me believe in the integrity of the earlier scriptures, and I then went on to answer Atif's point of view. I began by admitting that those passages did show that a change had taken place, but not in the scriptures themselves, not in the words that came from God.

The change was mainly in the interpretation of the text. Some people, specially the Jews around Muhammad in Madina, were accused of perverting the Word of God. Muslim scholars say that the way the Jews perverted was to misquote the text of the Torah in the presence of Muhammad or his companions. Others say that they used to misquote and misinterpret the sayings of Muhammad and the revelation of the Qur'an and that it is in this context that they are accused of '[displacing] words from their right places' and saying what the Word of God did not say. Now this is very different from changing the Word of God itself and one may conclude that these verses of the Qur'an deal with interpretation and indoctrination and not with the question of changing the word of God literally which is impossible to change or alter.

I added further that I found in the Qur'an that the contrary to Atif's assertion was true. I had discovered that it is impossible to change the Word of God, for it belongs to the unchanging, omnipotent God. I used the following texts to illustrate my point:

Rejected were the Apostles before thee: with patience and constancy they bore their rejection and their wrongs, until Our aid did reach them: there is none that can alter the Words (and Decrees) of God (Surah 6:34).

The Word of thy Lord doth find its fulfilment in truth and in justice: none can change His Words: for He is the one Who heareth and knoweth all (Surah 6:116).

For them are glad tidings, in the life of the present and in the hereafter: no change can there be in the Words of God (Surah 10:65).

We have, without doubt, sent down the Message; and We will assuredly guard it (from corruption) (Surah 15:9).

From these texts I learned the immutability of the word of God. If we say that the Torah has been changed, we infer the undoubted possibility that the Injil as well as the Qur'an have also been changed. And this is blasphemy, because it is dishonouring the Almighty God who promised 'We will assuredly guard it (from corruption).'

God forbid that he himself, the Lord of the worlds, should permit 'corruption' to enter the Torah or the Injil. How could it be possible that God who was able to protect the Qur'an from corruption was incapable of preserving the earlier scriptures from alteration? Such a belief would be sheer blasphemy! If we claim that the Torah and the Injil, which are both the word of God, have been changed by human beings, we have to admit that the Qur'an could have suffered the same indignity. Where would that leave our faith in the word of God?

I remembered how Atif and I were unable to continue a meaningful conversation as two more students had arrived and started hassling both of us.

It seemed as if that conversation had taken place only yesterday.

3

The Message

When I arrived home late that evening, I was glad to see that the water pressure was sufficient to fill the house water tank – unusually, the corner café was closed. And so after a nice shower, I made myself an omelette. I laid the table in the open yard near my bedroom window. Thanking God for his provision was nothing new for me. Even as a Muslim I had prayed before eating. In fact, all Muslims, as they stretch out their hand for food, recite, some aloud and others quietly, *'Bismallah arahman ar-rahim,'* (In the name of God, the Beneficent, the Most merciful). This prayer is part of the Qur'an and is the opening verse of every chapter or Surah except one.

After washing up, I sat in the open yard looking at the sky. Although the weather during the day had been humid and sticky, the night breeze was refreshing. I was thankful to have a shelter over my head. Most landlords do not consider bachelors to be good tenants, but my landlord was kind and understanding. This small one-bedroom house was located on a slight elevation in a suburb of Karachi. I was seated on a chair at a little table. As I turned, my vision was carried upward to the crystal-clear firmament above, studded with the sparkling stars of heaven. Though the moon was almost at its full, I still could see a lot of stars.

Both Muslims and Christians believe that God created the earth and the heavens and everything it contains. It is God who created Adam (*A'dem*) and Eve (*Hawa*). They believe that they lived in the paradise of God. However, due to a single but a serious act of disobedience, God caused them to leave it (Surah 2:36; 7:24–25; Genesis 3:23–24). Still, he did not leave Adam and Eve alone. He revealed himself from time to time to the children of Adam, their children and their children's children and so on, to lead them into the Straight Way, *Sirat al-Mustaqim*. Though God chose many people to convey His message to others, it was always with the single purpose, that of the people's salvation, *Najah*.

I remembered how, one evening, Atif and I had quite a long discussion on the person of God and his providence. As a Muslim, Atif felt uneasy when I called God 'our Father'.

'Masood! Why do Christians call God their Father?' He abruptly asked. 'God is so holy that we should not use procreating words for him. Christians are such a nice people yet they use such religious terms which are embarrassing and a stumbling block.'

His reaction was no different from many other Muslims who have similar questions when they come to know about Christians calling God their 'Father', and about Jesus, his prophet being called his 'Son'. I remembered the first time when as a twelve-year-old boy, I read a portion of the Christian Scriptures, the next day my first question to my teacher was: 'Is God our Father?' Perturbed by the question he enquired how on earth I could ask such a question and I had to tell him the whole story, how I happened to have got a Gospel according to John in the Urdu language. He kindly took me home and told me more about why God was not our Father and why we could not call him our Father.

In spite of that, several years later here I was as a believer calling God our Father (along with many other attributes) and Atif was asking me, 'Why do Christians call God as Father? How can God be a father when he has no wife, no son?'

To reject the idea of God being our Father, Atif straight away referred to the Qur'an. In his very impressive tone, he recited to me the following in Arabic:

> The originator of heavens and earth! How can He have a child, when there is for Him no consort, when He created all things and is aware of all things? (Surah 6:102).

> And (we believe) that He – exalted be the glory of our Lord! – hath taken neither wife nor son (Surah 72:3).

Hearing his quotations from the Qur'an, I said, 'I accept the Qur'anic argument.'

He was surprised when I said that I did not believe in the type of Fatherhood of God and the sonship of Jesus as condemned by the Qur'an. I could see he was fully alert to what I was saying and became more interested when I told him that the Bible nowhere spoke of God as having a wife and later a Son. Such an idea is not only repulsive but blasphemous.

He asked me, 'Why then use the term 'Son of God' for Jesus when you know it can lead to misunderstandings?'

The only answer I could give to him was, 'Would it be wise to abandon the use of a term that has the full approval of Jesus in the scriptures?'

'Where?' Atif quickly asked.

'Here is a discussion that one day took place between Jesus and his dear companions.' I opened the New Testament section of the Bible and read to him:

> When Jesus came to the region of Caesarea Philippi, he asked his disciples, 'Who do people say the Son of Man is?'
> They replied, 'Some say John the Baptist; others say Elijah; and still others, Jeremiah or one of the Prophets.'
> 'But what about you?' he asked. 'Who do you say I am?'
> Simon Peter answered, 'You are the Christ, the Son of the living God.'
> Jesus replied, 'Blessed are you, Simon son of Jonah, for this was not revealed to you by man, but my Father in heaven' (Matthew 16:13–17).

I shared with him that it was not the only place where God was addressed as Father and Jesus as the Son. I added, 'One may find these titles in several other passages in the Bible.'

I continued that when the angel gave glad tidings of a son to Mary, she said, 'How will this be, since I am a virgin?' The angel answered, 'The Holy Spirit will come upon you and the power of the Most High will overshadow you. So the holy one to be born will be called the Son of God' (Luke 1:34–35).

Atif quickly stopped me, 'Wait a minute! Don't rush!' He said, 'Surely the birth of Jesus and his role is unique both in Islam and Christianity, but don't forget that the Qur'an clearly says that Jesus is like Adam. As Adam was created by God, so was Jesus.'

He quoted the Qur'anic passage, 'Lo! The likeness of Jesus with Allah is as the likeness of Adam. He created him of dust, then He said unto Him: Be! And he is' (Surah 3:59).

He was further surprised when I said that I did believe in Jesus as a second Adam. According to the Scriptures, Jesus called himself also as 'the Son of Man' precisely because he was the second Adam. As Adam was created by God as perfect, so was Jesus in being the second Adam, sent through Mary into this world. They both have played important role in our lives. The Bible states:

> The first man Adam became a living being; the last Adam, a life giving spirit. The spiritual did not come first, but the natural, and after that the spiritual. The first man was of the dust of the earth, the second man from heaven (1 Corinthians 15:45–49).

Through Adam we have received a natural human body because of his earthly essence. However, Jesus had an earthly essence but also a heavenly essence so, by believing in him we can enter the spiritual realm. Jesus' essence is heavenly because he was with God as his Word.

Atif quickly interrupted, 'But the Qur'an says that those who say God is the Messiah, Jesus the son Mary, are disbelievers (Surah 5:17, 72) and assuming that Jesus in his essence lived with God is blasphemy. Isn't it so?'

'Surely it will be', I replied, 'if we only believed that the human being called Jesus son of Mary became God.

Christians address Jesus as the Son of God because of his coexistence with God before coming to this earth. We do not fully know how he co-existed with God, but one thing is very clear in the Bible: no one has seen God but it is Jesus who reveals him and what he is like. The Bible testifies in these words:

> The Word became flesh and lived for a while among us. We have seen his glory, the glory of the one and only Son, who came from the Father, full of grace and truth (John 1:14).

This passage from the Bible tells us that Jesus is the eternal Word of God. He is the one who can reveal God to us because he was with God from the beginning:

> In the beginning was the Word, and the Word was with God, and the Word was God. He was with God in the beginning (John 1:1–2).

It is easy to understand that, since God is eternal, then his Word must also be eternal. No one on this earth has been called the Word of God or the word from him, *Kalimatan minhu*, other than Jesus (Surah 3:45). If the majority of Muslims can accept the idea that God gave expression to his eternal Word in the form of eternal Qur'an, then it is also possible to accept that God gave expression to his eternal Word in the form of Christ. The Word became incarnate as the Son of Man.

I stopped and waited for Atif's response but he said, 'Oh! I am little confused. Perhaps, I need to inquire more and study these things carefully.'

Scribbling quickly into his notebook, he said, 'And by the way, please don't run a thousand miles an hour when you try to explain your point of view to me. I am not a *Moulvi* from the Grand Mosque on an equal footing with you.'

I apologised and promised to be careful next time.

Sitting there that evening I realised that I missed Atif a lot. A terrible bite of some mosquito or insect brought me back from memory lane. I also saw that on the wall the same big cat I had seen that morning had returned and was sitting in ambush for another attack on the chickens next door. To chase it away, I waved my hands. It slowly moved away looking at me as though saying, 'Don't chase me. I too need to eat to survive.'

4

Joy and Suffering

Like many other co-workers I was late. The unexpected wildcat strike by the public transport known as *Pahiyya jam* had caused many to find other means of transport to reach their place of work or other destinations. The only people in my department who arrived on time were those who had their own means of transport.

Due to other reasons, the flight schedules were also running late so we received only a few deliveries to and from European destinations. After about three hours of work there was nothing else to do. To pass the time some workers started chatting and sipping tea, while others, as usual, excused themselves to have an early lunch followed by the afternoon prayer. Two made an excuse and took some detained pornographic and other printed material to the deputy's office on the third floor. In the whole hall only I and another colleague were left. After a chat about all sorts of issues except religion, he started dozing off, with a half-finished cigarette in his hand. I took it from him before it started a fire of the mail bags on the floor next to him.

Because I also worked as part of the censorship team my duty was also to read. As usual I picked some Christian magazines addressed to some internal

destination and started browsing. After a while the
afternoon post arrived and a letter was there for me. It
was from a dear Christian friend, Mr Smith, with
whom I had recorded some Christian radio
programmes. He asked me if I could go urgently and
help him so that programmes could be aired on time.
Here was something I really wanted to do. I was glad
because, according to the office schedule for the following week, I was to have my remaining week of
annual leave; and I had nothing else to do.

Two days later there I was on my way on the long
train journey to the Northwest frontier region of Pakistan. It was summer and the rains had still not come.
As usual the dust was thick in the air as I left the bus
and walked towards the railway station. The huge
brick building was thronged with people, even at that
early hour, as the trains came and went all over the
country.

Clutching my bag tightly, I strode over to the timeta-
ble and found that a train was leaving shortly for
Lahore, Rawalpindi and Peshawar. I took my place in
the long queue. Through the small ticket window I
paid the fare and, without any question, he gave me the
ticket, an oblong piece of cardboard stamped with the
name of my destination – Rawalpindi. Perhaps he
knew from the amount of my money that I wanted to
go to Rawalpindi.

The big diesel engine came alongside the platform,
pulling its great length of carriages and, as usual, a
flood of people poured in through every opening. In
the unreserved carriages, for which I had my ticket,
everyone scrambled for a place. People threw their
baggage through the unbarred windows and there

were many loud and heated arguments before all were accommodated. At last, I was glad to find some room on a bench near a half-shut window, through which it had been impossible for people to insert their luggage.

After a long delay, during which the carriage became as hot as an oven and the drink vendors found a thirsty market for their wares, the train started on its thirty-six hour journey toward the north in a slow motion – even slower than the slow boat to China. The carriages were old and in poor repair. I closed my eyes and spoke a few words of thanks to our creator for being alive and pleading with him to grant peace to us all during the journey.

At first the squeaks and screeches underneath the floor made me uncomfortable but soon my ears became used to the noise. Old memories kept flooding back. I had made several journeys on this track before, sometimes not even knowing where I was heading and what the destination held for me. This time, however, I knew I had to get off at Rawalpindi and then take a bus to Murree, a hill station that many people frequented during the hot summer season.

At Lahore, my mind was full of the memories of past events. I remembered that Lahore was where a few students boarded the train thinking that I was going to Murree Hills, and invited me to share lodging with them – I accepted and eventually met Mr Smith who needed somebody to take part in his Christian broadcast. It is surprising how links and connection between friends are made in this world, and I thanked the Lord for making us to be in need of each other, thereby bringing us understanding, love and affection.

The train reached Rawalpindi late the next evening.

It is an impressive city. I decided to find a cheap hotel
to spend the night. I would start early the next day for
Murree, going the further thirty-five miles by road.
After an hour's search, I was able to find a reasonable
room to stay. In the next hour, I had a good shower to
rid myself of the dust which seemed to become part of
my face and hands.

After that, I had something to eat from a small restaurant, and then I decided to have a little walkabout.
Many of the businesses and retail shops were closed.
Only restaurants and cinemas remained open. After a
mile's walk I returned to my hotel room. As usual, I
read a portion of the scriptures, contemplated, and
thanked God for all his providence, and tried to sleep.

Although I had travelled for almost thirty-six hours,
somehow I could not sleep. I dragged myself out and
sat on the rocking chair on the balcony. I could see the
street lights and neon signs on the sides of adjacent
buildings. I saw the train station where a train had just
arrived. One of the red carriages was for the postal services. I remembered how Atif and I had travelled in
one of these carriages during our training in the postal
services. It was certainly quite a difficult task for us as
beginners to read addresses on the letters and then
throw them into the right pigeon boxes, to be put in the
mail bags for the oncoming stations from where other
postal workers could take them to the local sorting
offices.

I remembered how once the whole train was stuck
for two days because a flood had washed away the
track at both ends. We were fortunate in an area where
the rail track was on higher ground. Many people had
made their own ways, but we had to stay with the

postal carriage for some time.

While several of us talked about other issues or played cards and other games, I and Atif had talked more about our faith, our beliefs and our concerns. Somehow the issue of suffering came to the fore. One of our colleagues, who claimed to be a practising Muslim and performed each of his five daily prayers on time, was most concerned about the flood. He heard us talking about calamities, and interrupted us saying, 'It is God's revenge on wicked people. Famine, wars, earthquakes, floods and other calamities strike humanity as a final warning from Allah so that people may repent.'

Atif disagreed and argued that good and bad, the innocent and the wicked, all face suffering. How could one say that every wrong thing happens because of somebody's wickedness?

Then why do people suffer? Why does God allow suffering? We went on and on but at last came to an understanding that we may suffer because of our own faults and sin. Although my Muslim colleague did not like me quoting from the Bible, he agreed with what it says, 'A man reaps what he sows' (Galatians 6:7). People may also suffer because of the effect of the wrongdoings of others. At times, God allows innocent people to suffer, like Job (Surah 38:41). Some who had never seen the Bible were surprised to see a full story related in the Bible in the book of Job.

Then someone said, 'If both bad and good, righteous and unrighteous suffer equally, then this is not right.'

To put the matter straight, I quickly responded, 'Yes, both may suffer and lose their lives in this world but while the unrighteous have no hope or assurance for eternal life, the righteous have hope in God. Both the Qur'an and the Bible testify to this truth (Surah 4:104). The Bible confirms that while bad or unrighteous will taste eternal destruction, the righteous will dwell in the fellowship of God forever' (Revelation 7:15–7).

We were also coming to a realisation that often God allows suffering so that people may learn a lesson as it says in the Qur'an: 'And We sent no prophet unto any township but We did afflict its folk with tribulation and adversity that haply they might grow humble' (Surah 7:94).

I read to them from the Bible that one day Jesus and his disciples (*Hawariun*) saw a blind man. They asked Jesus, 'Rabbi, who sinned, this man or his parents, that he was born blind?'

'Neither this man nor his parents sinned', said Jesus, 'but this happened so that the work of God might be displayed in his life.'

Jesus then healed the man. The next day, the man testified about Jesus before the spiritual leaders of the Jews, 'Nobody has ever heard of opening the eyes of a man born blind. If this man were not from God, he could do nothing' (John 9:2–34).

I added that sometimes we suffer hardship as a form of discipline from God. The Bible says, 'No discipline seems pleasant at the time, but painful. Later on, however, it produces a harvest of righteousness and peace for those who have been trained by it' (Hebrews 12:11).

All those sitting there agreed that, according to the teaching of both the Bible and the Qur'an, God is not obliged to state reasons for his sovereign actions. Occasionally he allows information to filter through so that we learn the cause of someone's sufferings. No matter what happens to us and our fellow men and women in this world, in the light of the scriptures we learn that for those who have submitted themselves to God, in the hereafter certainly, God 'will wipe every tear from their eyes. There will be no more death or mourning or crying or pain' (Revelation 21:4).

By this time only Atif and I were left alone and we talked for such a long time that next morning the duty supervisor took me to one side and advised me not to hold discussions on religious issues and warned that his complaint could land both Atif and me in trouble when we returned.

The next afternoon, one side of the track had been reconnected and the train was diverted to Rohri Junction. Though still far from our destination, we were glad to be safe. When a flood comes, it takes several days to overcome the disruption to traffic between cities. It is no wonder that it took us several more days to arrive back in Karachi. However, for Atif and me, the flood was also a blessing. We became more than friends, we were like brothers. He asked me if he could borrow my copy of the Bible for a few days and I gladly surrendered it.

The noise of a big bang shook me. I quickly got to my feet and looked down the road. A truck's tyre had burst. I looked at the railway station. Only a few people were sitting on the platform; the train with the postal carriage that I had seen earlier had left already.

I went back into the room, switched on the fan to a low speed to keep away the mosquitoes and tucked myself under the sheet. When I opened my eyes it was morning. I was thankful for some sleep in spite of such noise. Eager to be on my way I repacked my bag and got ready. In no time I had checked out of the hotel and found my way to the bus station. I reached the cool of Murree about three hours later.

Murree is built on a series of ridges and all the vegetation is of cold weather varieties. There is often snow in winter but even at this time of the year the place was full of people each wearing new wool sweaters and even gloves and coats, though it was not really cold. For Pakistanis who live in constant heat on the plains, Murree can seem cold.

The Mall was the centre of attraction with many little shops on either side, and over it all was the spire of the Union Church – a grey stone building that reminded us that the British had first established Murree as a cool place for themselves. A language school was also run in the grounds of Union Church. It was the principal of this language school who had introduced me to Mr Smith two years before and, since then, we had become good friends.

The main *bazaar* had not changed much and I made my way to the post office to phone Mr Smith. He was delighted at my arrival and took me to the place where he stayed and where his makeshift studio was. He was also saddened by the news of Atif's sudden death. He had met Atif just six months previously when he visited Karachi. That evening we all remembered Atif and prayed that God would grant peace to the hearts of his brother and mother.

The next few days were busy as we finished some twenty quarter-hour Christian programmes, each in the Pushtu language. It was hard work but a real labour of love; I enjoyed every minute of it. The area in which I stayed was on a high hill. From my room on a clear day I could see the valley below. In the evening I would sit near the window or walk out into the cold night under the glittering stars. I would sit there for a long time looking at the colourful display of lights in the valley.

On the day I left, Mr Smith showed me some photographs he took during his visit to Atif and me and gave me two to keep as a memento. His family had invited some other guests, of whom two were on the way back to Finland. I was thankful that everything finished as planned. I was very much at peace knowing that I had done all that God had brought me to do in Murree. The question still remained, however, whether I was looking forward to seeing the city of Karachi again where just a few days earlier a very dear friend had been buried.

Instead of taking the train, I flew back to Karachi as the roads and trains were closed due to the flood. Mr Smith very kindly paid this for me. I wondered often during the flight how many would listen to the programmes we recorded. How would they respond to the good news of what God has done for us all, and that he does not want anyone to perish but to be saved and have eternal life? … I prayed a lot for all of them.

On my arrival in Karachi, I took a *riksha*, a three-wheeler taxi, from the airport through the old familiar roads and streets. I felt lonely when I entered my flat. I thought about my mother and father, and my own brothers and sisters who had disowned me because I had become a follower of Jesus, a Christian.

That night when I opened the Bible for my daily reading the words of Jesus brought great peace to my aching heart:

> Anyone who loves his father or mother more than me is not worthy of me; and anyone who loves his son or daughter more than me is not worthy of me; and anyone who does not take his cross and follow me is not worthy of me. Whoever finds his life will lose it and whoever loses his life for my sake will find it. He who receives you receives me, and he who receives me receives the one who sent me (Matthew 10:36–38).

5

What's in a Name?

It was the last day for my enrolment registration for the BA exams at the university. My documents were in order but the clerk at the counter was more concerned about the change of my name and religion, although they did not affect my application. However, he asked me to produce some type of official pronouncement by way of a public declaration. All that morning, I was pushed from one office to another but never received certain answers. To my dismay, when I finally returned to the counter to tell the clerk my story, I found another clerk sitting in his place. The first had gone to perform his prayers. To my surprise, the other clerk accepted all my documents and issued me a receipt in acknowledgement along with my registration number.

I could see that the first clerk who was very religious – he had probably tried to practise Islam to the letter – was in fact making excuses not to accept me as a candidate just because I had changed my faith and thus changed my name too. By contrast, the second clerk, who was also a Muslim, was more open in both heart and mind.

I was heartened by this acceptance; now I could go

back and continue with my studies. I still had mixed feelings because Atif and I had decided to appear in the exam together. We had even chosen the same subjects but, he was no longer there.

I returned to work by bus; I had been granted only half a day's leave and I was already an hour late. My supervisor was not very happy and continued to scold me. I was afraid that another charge sheet was going to be on its way to me. I constantly asked for God's help and strength and, to everyone's surprise, I found that I was able to finish the due checking, sorting and packing of the mail bags just in time before the collecting officer arrived at the door.

The supervisor was somewhat suspicious. He checked and rechecked with the help of the collecting officer, but could find no excuse to haul me in for a charge sheet. He smilingly said, *'Kab tak bachoge!'*, (For how long will you escape!) I did not say anything and continued filing the carbon copies left by the collecting officer.

To my surprise, Atif's brother, Hassan, came to see me and, as a further surprise, I found that he and the supervisor had been class-fellows during their college days. Hassan told me that he had come to collect Atif's belongings from his locker. He gave me a bag which he thought contained a few things that perhaps had been mine. I thankfully received the bag from him.

After some tea and a good chat Hassan, before leaving, came to me and invited me to attend Atif's *Cheh'lum* (the funeral rite performed on the fortieth day after death). He was certainly reluctant but, since his mother had insisted, he invited me to attend.

It was quite late in the evening that day when I arrived home. After eating my dinner at the corner café and finishing the usual bits and pieces and other necessary things at home, I was at last able to relax to sit, read or listen to the tapes or radio. That evening, I switched on the radio but for some unknown reason, the Christian radio from the Seychelles could not be heard. I finally switched it off after several unsuccessful efforts.

Then I remembered the brown bag that Hassan had given me. I quickly got it from the table where I had left it earlier. There were a few books, the Bible and some papers with notes in Atif's handwriting. I also found a few pages of a response I had written to answer his queries. I paged through the Bible and found that he had written several comments in the margins of some pages which gave me the clue that he had become a very serious seeker to find the truth.

'But why would he leave his things in his office closet and not at his home?' I wondered. His mother was not a person who would be upset about his study. The only concern was his brother but, again, he too was liberal in his Islamic approach to such things.

In the New Testament section of the Bible, I saw that Atif had marked a passage where Jesus had once said to a woman, 'I was sent only to the lost sheep of the house of Israel' (Matthew 15:24).

In the margin Atif's question read, 'Was he only for Israel?' He had also added some cross-references where the ministry of Jesus was mentioned to be for all. His question reminded me of our discussion of those days when he somehow wanted to cling on to any excuse which could help him to prove that the message brought by Jesus was just for a time and for certain people only.

I remembered how one afternoon he quoted and argued to prove to me the limits of Jesus' ministry. I pointed out that such a notion was even against the Qur'an where he is described as 'a sign to all the worlds, *ayatan lil-alamin*' and 'a sign to man-kind, *ayatan lin-nas*' (Surah 21:91; 19:21). If Jesus was only a messenger for the Jews, he could not be a sign for all people of the world.

Though after some discussion, Atif agreed that Jesus was more than a messenger and did not belong to just one community, he was still persistent that the message brought by Jesus was purely for the Jews and not for others. I had to point out to him that one of the best principles of interpreting was to check as many references on the subject and then draw an outcome.

'There are several other passages', I added, 'where we do find that the ministry of Jesus was a universal one (John 8:12, Matthew 12:15–21; Isaiah 42:1ff). If his mission was restricted only to the Jews, he could not have given the great commission before his ascension: "Go and make disciples of all nations" (Matthew 28:19). The companions of Jesus understood his command to preach to all nations. They obeyed because they knew that the gospel of Jesus "is the power of God for the salvation of everyone who believes: first for the Jews, then for the Gentiles" (Roman 1:16).'

'If that is the case', Atif argued, 'then why did Jesus say that he had been sent only to "the lost sheep of Israel"?'

I paused and, collecting my thought, I said that as long as Jesus was on earth, he limited his ministry and that of his disciples to the Israelites (Matthew 8:10).

But, at the time of his ascension into heaven he ordered his companions to take the message far and wide to all nations. So, his message was not simply for the Jews but also for many outside. God had promised Abraham that he would bless all nations through him (Genesis 18:18).

I remembered sharing with Atif how the Bible relates how Jesus one day told his audience that, 'Abraham rejoiced at the thought of seeing my day; he saw it and was glad' (John 8:56).

Indeed this was the promise to which Jesus referred when he said, 'I have other sheep which are not of this fold; I must bring them also ... and there shall be one flock and one shepherd' (John 10:16). The words 'which are not of this fold' refer to non-Jews.

Certainly I was glad to see that Atif had written those references in the margin of his Bible concerning the passages where the ministry of Jesus is mentioned for all.

Also in his Bible was a small piece of paper stuck between the beginning of John and the end of the gospel according to Luke. The paper seemed to refer to the first few verses where Jesus is mentioned as the Word of God. Atif had written some appellations:

Adam: *Safiy'y-ullah*, God's elect;
Abraham, *Khalilullah*, the friend of God;
Moses, *Kalim-ullah*, God's interlocutor;
Jesus, *Kalamat-ullah wa Ruh-allah*, God's word and spirit.
If God is eternal, that means that his *word*, Jesus, is also eternal.

It was all amazing. Certainly he must have been studying very carefully. Muslims usually do not like

scribbling in the scriptures but Atif seemed to be different. He was more interested to find not only the truth
but the whole truth.

In one of my earlier meetings with him, he was very
upset with me for not using honorific words for Jesus
whenever I mentioned his name. I had to give him several reasons why Christians do not use words like,
'Alaihis salam, peace be upon him' whenever they mention the name of Jesus. It took him no time to understand that since Jesus himself is the source and giver of
peace, there is no need to send on him 'Peace'. It is we
who need his peace. And he gives that peace to us. He
said, 'My peace I give you. I do not give as the world
gives' (John 14:27). He has promised us eternal peace.
This was the main reason why the companions of
Jesus, while meeting others or writing to others, said,
'Grace and peace to you from God and our Lord Jesus
the Christ' (Ephisians 1:2; Galatians 1:3; Titus 1:4).

I was amazed to see Atif's hand-written statement
referring to an Old Testament passage (Isaiah 9:6),
'Masih, Salamati ka Shahzadha, Christ, the Prince of
Peace.' I thought of the many people who, like Atif,
must be searching for the ultimate reality and yet are
careful not to arouse suspicion and be declared as
doubters and apostates by fellow Muslims. I asked
myself, can one be 'a secret believer'? Some believe that
Nicodemus, mentioned in the Gospel according to
John, was a secret believer. Once in the dark of the
night, he visited Jesus to know him more. However,
even he identified himself as a follower or perhaps a
sympathiser when Jesus' body was brought to be buried
(John 3:1ff; 7:50; 19:39).

That night before going to sleep, I knelt down and

prayed for the many out there searching for the truth about Jesus.

6

Assurance

I came home very late at the end of each of the following three evenings. A convention had been arranged in one of the church. It was heart warming to attend, to sing hymns, listen to the reading of the scripture and to hear men and women of God sharing their testimonies of how God helped them in their daily lives. It was also nice to see my friends.

Mr Massey was one of those people who had always helped me to know more about Jesus. It was during the last evening of the convention that we saw each other among the many people attending the meeting. He was extremely glad to see me. We talked about many things. I could not stop the tears as he asked me how Atif was; he had met him on several occasions with me. I told him about Atif's sudden death. We both wept, but the only thing we could do was to pray for peace and security for his family. We talked about how Atif was curious to know more about the Christian faith. When I returned home that night, my mind was still full of that evening's events.

I could hear from two streets away from my home that a kind of singing function was occurring, and the amplified noise prevented me from sleeping much. I admired the neighbours' patience for not complaining.

I was still sleepy the next day when I arrived at work. There had apparently been many delays in the arrivals and departures, caused by a pay dispute between the airport workers and the management. Our office day was therefore mostly spent sipping tea and chatting with each other.

Some at work tried to taunt me by starting religious discussions, but I resisted because I remembered how previously Atif, friends and I had been reprimanded for talking in the office canteen. I was specifically warned that if I wanted to be a missionary, then I could go somewhere else.

I felt so on my own as I sat there in my chair. Around me were co-workers, yet I felt far from them. During these past few days, they had started calling me a day-dreamer, philosopher and Master Thinker. I did not mind that. Through the days, months and years, I thought how much my behaviour had changed. I seemed to have been living a day-to-day type of life. The future was a concern but not much of a worry any-more. The day-to-day happenings of each day were different. The unpredictability and unexpected out-come of events did not comfort me. There was only one thing I was sure of: that believing in Jesus was the only way ahead. I believed that I was saved, that I am being saved and that, on the day of judgement, I will be saved from eternal destruction.

'How about those who haven't believed in Jesus? What about them?' I remembered a colleague shouting at me when Atif and I were sharing our thoughts over cups of teas in a corner of the canteen.

My answer was that it was up to God to know and

decide but as far as I knew, the Bible clearly said, 'Whoever believes in Jesus, will surely have eternal life.'
There is an assurance available.

'But the same can be said of the Qur'an.' I remembered Atif interrupting, 'Those who believe in God and
the Prophet (Muhammad) and do good deeds – God
will grant them paradise.'

He continued, 'The Qur'an promises that on the day
of judgement, the Prophet, peace be upon him, will be
our intercessor. We, as Muslims, though guilty of some
sins, will at the end of the day be forgiven because of
the Prophet's intercession. What would you say to
that?'

I remembered there were some twelve people
around me sitting looking at me with questioning
faces. I felt as though I was in the middle of some dual.
In my heart, in a split second I seemed to scream,
'Please God, help me!'

'Come on! Answer!' Someone tapped the table.

'As far as I have learned from the Qur'an', I started,
'the assurance of forgiveness, and Muhammad being
an intercessor on the day of judgement, cannot be
proved from the Qur'an which is the first-hand authority in such matters.'

'Liar! Liar!' someone shouted.

'Let him finish', Atif asked them. 'Please be quiet.'

'What I have found in the Qur'an', I said, choosing
my words very carefully, 'is that a Muslim is not sure
whether he will have any forgiveness or not. In fact the
Qur'an in some passages claims that God has created
some for hell and some for paradise (Surah 11:118;
16:93; 19:71,72). It is not the Prophet of Islam but God
who will decide whom he wishes to send to paradise or

to hell on the day of judgement. Thus a Muslim may perform all his *Salah* and give *Zakah* and do righteous deeds but, at the end, he is not sure in this life whether or not he has earned forgiveness. Even the Prophet of Islam was not sure. In the Qur'anic language, his words to many were, "I am no new thing among the messengers (of Allah), nor know I what will be done with me or with you..." ' (Surah 46:9).

'You mean that the Qur'an does not say in clear words that Muhammad will be our intercessor on the day of Judgement?' Atif asked me.

'Yes! That is what I have found so far,' I replied hesitantly.

'Rubbish! I will tell you! I am going to find out.' Atif felt furious but was in control of himself. He went on to say, 'And this understanding of yours that God has already created some for hell and some for paradise, if that is true then why did God send 124,000 prophets into this world to lead people into his straight path?'

'Surely that was my dilemma too before I became a Christian', I responded.

'What do you mean?' a colleague nearby shouted.

I replied, 'On the one hand, we see the belief in Islam that God has sent his messengers to give us guidance and yet, on the other, the Qur'an says that God 'misleadeth who he pleases and guideth who he pleases' (Surah 14:4). In contrast, I found in the Bible that God is not like that. He is patient, 'not wanting anyone to perish, but everyone to come to repentance' (2 Peter 3:9).

I felt persuaded to share with them what I had found and thus I began to say, 'In this life, the Prophet of Islam is mentioned as having said that he did not know what was going to happen to him or his *Ummah*, community. Yet I was surprised to see Jesus in the Christian Scriptures that he knew where he came from and where he was going (John 8:14). He even told his followers before his departure that he was going back to the heavens of God to prepare a place for them (John 14:2–3).'

Quoting from the scriptures, I added that Jesus boldly claimed:

Come to me and I will give you rest (Matthew 11:28).

If you want to be perfect … come, follow me (Matthew 19:21).

I am the resurrection and the life. He who believes in me will live, even though he dies (John 11:25).

I am the way and the truth and the life (John 14:6).

I then added that Jesus claimed that people could only come into the presence of God through him.

A co-worker standing near to Atif said, 'So, as a Christian, you just have to believe in him and no matter what you do you will have *Jan'nah*, paradise? No wonder, the West which is predominantly Christian is so morally corrupt because their corrupted book does not teach them to do good deeds.'

Somebody else also interrupted but I asked if I might reply, and then continued: 'This is a parody and contradictory to the teaching of Jesus and of his companions. As Christians, we not only have to do good but in fact our doing good must be more; and it should not be done merely to gain praise from people' (Matthew 5:20; 6:1).

I remembered a passage in the scripture and quickly got my small pocket Urdu edition of the New Testament. I said, 'Let me read to you a passage among many that are here.' It was a passage that I had read that very morning and without waiting I read it to them:

> For the grace of God that brings salvation has appeared to all men. It teaches us to say 'No' to ungodliness and worldly passions, and to live self-controlled, upright and godly lives in this present age, while we wait for the blessed hope – the glorious appearing of our great God and Saviour, Jesus Christ, who gave himself for us to redeem us from all wickedness and to purify for himself a people that are his very own, eager to do what is good (Titus 2:11–14).

I continued by saying that the commandment is not only to be doing good but also helping others to do good.

> Remind the people to be subject to rulers and authorities, to be obedient, to be ready to do whatever is good, to slander no-one, to be peaceable and considerate, and to show true humility towards all men (Titus 3:1–2).

I closed the book and said, 'Belief is an essential part of a Christian's faith. However, if one claims to believe in Jesus but does not follow what he has said, then there is no truth in that person. If someone claims to love God then this love should compel him to do what God has commanded. In other words, to abstain from actions and deeds which will make him unhappy. This submissive action on a Christian's part is not to gain a seat in paradise but it is in response to that love and first initiative that Jesus took for us and towards us.'

There was a hush for a while. I looked at Atif and around, there was a quietness. Though it lasted only for a few seconds, it seemed like an eternity. Someone quietly asked to see the New Testament in my hand and I let him see it.

At last someone standing behind me broke the silence, 'O, Come on! Jesus was just an apostle of God. He wouldn't say such things.' He added, 'It is the Christians who have put such words in Jesus' mouth in order to exalt him to the level of God.'

'Friend! You have introduced another subject here', I confidently said. 'We were talking about forgiveness and intercession, and not the subject of the integrity of the Bible and the Qur'an. However, if you would prefer, we can discuss that too.'

'Why don't we all go to Moulvi Ahmad Yar', someone else suggested. Moulvi Ahmad Yar was an Imam of the mosque adjacent to the grounds of the Postal Services. I also nodded in response and asked that one of them would arrange. Atif reluctantly took the responsibility. Meanwhile, the assistant supervisor came in and was angry with us, and dispersed us to our respective places of work.

'Our philosopher has wandered off again', somebody shouted. I smiled and excused myself to get a cold drink. When I came back, a colleague asked me what was so special that my thoughts had been so far away and so sad. Before I could reply, though, another said, 'Well it is natural to be sad when you have lost a best friend.'

'You must have been thinking more than that. I could see some inquisitive expressions on your face.' Then I remembered that he was the man who had taken my pocket New Testament, and never returned it.

'You remember when we had that discussion in the canteen and you took the *Injil*, to look at it? I was thinking about that. Did you read it? Do you still have that copy? Would you like to return it?' Perhaps I asked him too many questions.

He apologised for not returning it, then said that he thought he had given it to another friend, who in turn had given it to someone else. While we were talking, the supervisor came near and addressed us like a dictator, '*Zuban say ziyada hath chalao.*' (Work with your hands not with your tongues.)

'And you!' He waved his finger towards me, '*Jalil Sahib* would like to have a word with you tomorrow morning. Report to his office at 11:00. I think you are out.' And he walked back to his office.

My colleagues and I looked at each other, but said nothing.

7

Things Ahead

At home that evening, I tried not to think about the day to come, but again and again it kept coming back to me. What would I be asked, and what would be my answer? The threats from the hierarchy were not new to me. I was somewhat concerned when the assistant supervisor told me that I had been away for a whole week without leave, and that perhaps my leave was the cause of it. However, I calmed myself with the knowledge that my copy of the letter accepting my leave could be shown to the Superintendent if any problems arose.

I was sure that, at present, I was there just to earn enough to live on. If the question had not been of survival, perhaps I would have left the job long ago. The cross-examination by co-workers, superiors and others at work was becoming worse. Their veiled taunts were often depressing. Perhaps, I thought, the Lord wanted me to be there. I had tried so far to trust him, and continued to be ready to endure what was ahead.

In the past I had done my utmost only to explain why I followed Jesus during the lunch break but, one day, I received a warning from my superior, the head of my division. He accused me of fostering sectarian discussions during office time, and advised me that I would lose my job if it did not stop. Furthermore, he warned me that if it came to such an end, I might well find myself prosecuted in the (civil) courts. Since then I had been very careful but I still received accusations of negligence in my work. Indeed I was twice charged with sending a bundle of letters to a wrong destination, whereas it could have been switched by any colleague or superior in order to punish me. And now, tomorrow was going to be something else. There was little I could do, yet I needed that job to survive.

Even the union leaders were not interested. One of their leaders had even threatened me saying that if I got into trouble it would all be my own fault, and that I should not expect the union's support. I replied that, as far as I was concerned, God is the union leader and that he would help me. The man and his friend just laughed at me. Yet this same man would sometimes ask some quite serious questions, so that I was able to share something of what Christ meant to me. The common denominator that bound them all was their fear of the Bible. At the end of any important discussion, they would go back to square one by claiming, 'Your Bible is corrupted. It is not the same gospel which Jesus gave to his companions.'

At times I asked colleagues at work and acquaintances at the university to at least take the scriptures and read them. Some agreed, but others refused and attacked it using Muslim sources, people who had written against the Bible and Christians. Despite all this, I was glad that there were those few who listened and Atif was chief among them. In this way, day after day, study, discussions and sometime, argumentative talks continued.

The crucial turning point for Atif was when he and his friend arranged an open meeting for me with Moulvi Ahmad Yar who had been briefed about the discussion we had at the cafeteria. It seemed that Moulvi Ahmad Yar had no quibble about what I had previously shared with friends. He did not even question the integrity of the Torah, the Psalms or the Injil, but concentrated on the argument that all these books which are found in the Bible are now *mansukh* – abrogated. He claimed that the Qur'an had replaced them all. He referred to a passage which says, 'Such of our revelations as We abrogate or cause to be forgotten, we bring (in place) one better or the like thereof' (Surah 2:105).

He continued by saying that the message brought by Muhammad, known as Islam, is for all people everywhere because the Qur'an says that Islam is the only religion which is acceptable to God.

It was something of a surprise to Atif and the others that I took notes of what Moulvi Yar Ahmad said. He had based his whole presentation on the Qur'an and the *Ahadith* traditions, and stated that in the light of the Qur'an not the Bible, people would be judged. He claimed that on his second coming, Jesus would also live as a follower of the holy Prophet of Allah, Muhammad, and would be a Muslim.

It took him little more than half an hour during which we listened respectfully. Atif then looked at me as if to ask for my response. I asked for permission to speak and requested that the *Moulvi Sahib* would ask those who were in attendance not to interrupt until I finish. I knew this was crucial because of my past experiences. Some of the listeners thought I was just making excuses and taunted me, *'Bacha! bahanay mat banawo, bolo, jawab do!'* (Child! Don't make excuses. Speak, respond!)

Choosing my apologetic words carefully, I responded, 'With due respect, may I say that the doctrine known as *Al-Naskh Wa Al-Mansukh*, the abrogation and the abrogated is not about the Bible. My study so far is that the Qur'an does not abrogate what was revealed before it in the Torah, the Psalms and the Injil. As the respected Imam was referring to the Qur'an, I will do the same.'

I continued, 'Many early *Muffasirin* and *Muhadithin* (Islamic commentators and scholars of traditions) are of the opinion that several verses in the present Qur'an have been abrogated and replaced by other verses. Other arguments suggest that certain verses of the Qur'an have been abrogated but no replacement verses were revealed or recorded. The extent of this is the subject of much controversy, varying from five verses to several hundred and such details can be found in good classical commentaries on the Qur'an by prominent Muslims.'

'We as the students of the history of Islam', I stated, 'are taught that when the Prophet of Islam was accused by his opponents of giving contradictory statements in the Qur'an, in result he received a revelation that Allah replaced some of the text of the Qur'an with a later text.'

I was glad to remember the passage and opened the Qur'an. Someone quickly interrupted that since I was now an apostate, I was therefore unclean and should not touch the Qur'an. Not to let the situation get out of hand, I agreed that someone should read. Atif agreed

and at my request read the passage in a recitation
mode:

> And when We put a revelation in place of (another)
> revelation, – and Allah knoweth best what He
> revealeth – they say: Lo! Thou art but inventing. Most
> of them know not (Surah 16:101).

'With all due respect may I say', I added, 'that even
looking, hearing and reciting this verse we see that it
does not state that Allah replaced one '*Kitab*' (book)
with another but rather that he substituted one *aya* for
another. The word *aya* in the context here refers only to
the verses of the Qur'an and not the book of the Christians or the Jews or their verses.'

'Further, I would like to say that the Qur'an, instead
of claiming abrogation of previous scriptures, in fact
claims to be, '*musadiqallima bayna yadahi* – confirming
what went before it (Surah 3:3), namely the Tawrat and
Injil. In the same Qur'an I find that both Jews and
Christians are instructed to abide and judge by their
scriptures.'

Further on, I added that if the Qur'an came to abrogate the Torah and Injil, it would not have asked the
Jews and Christians to abide by them. It would not
have been proper for the Qur'an to advise in these
words:

> How come they unto thee for judgement when they
> have the Torah, wherein Allah hath delivered judge-
> ment (for them)? (Surah 5:43).

> Let the People of the Gospel judge by that which Allah
> hath revealed therein. Whoso judgeth not by that which
> Allah hath revealed; such are evil-livers (Surah 5:47).

My audience seemed attentive and thus I continued: 'With regard to the idea that God accepts only Islam, may I say that the Qur'an claims that Abraham was a Muslim. In fact it is believed in Islam that Moses, David and Jesus all were Muslims. Why? Because each of them surrendered their lives to God. So we may conclude that anyone who believes in God and the day of Judgement, as the Qur'an says, will have no fear (Surah 2:62). Why? Because such people surrendered themselves and are thus Muslims. God sent so many prophets and apostles, but the message has always been the same; *surrender to God*.'

'Even Jesus while on this earth preached this message. Indeed his prayer was, "Not my will but may your will be done." He advised his companions to pray that as God's will is fulfilled in heaven, may it also be fulfilled on earth.

I thus concluded, similarly, all true followers of Jesus, Moses and Abraham could be said to be Muslims and their belief could be called Islam.

'*Kufr*, *Kufr*, blasphemy, blasphemy,' someone shouted, but the Imam did not show any anger. He instead asked the audience to be quiet and began by saying, 'Your reasoning is childish but I have to say that we, as Muslims, do not need the earlier scriptures because the Qur'an also contains the earlier scriptures.'

I asked him reverently if he would show me where and he referred to the story of Adam, Noah, Abraham, Joseph, Moses, David and Jesus and so on. When he finished, I was given the chance to respond. I had to ask again where the Qur'an had said that it contained the previous scriptures, the Torah and the Gospel. In fact the Qur'an claims that it is found in the earlier books of the former people (Surah 26:196). Furthermore the Qur'an claims to have come lest the Arabs make excuses that they cannot understand the languages in which the earlier books, the Torah and the Gospel, were revealed (Surah 5:157,158).

Moreover, a Muslim is required to believe in the books of the prophets and make no distinction between them. Here the whole idea of abrogation of the earlier scriptures becomes wholly contradictory to the teaching of the Qur'an because it demands that Muslims declare, 'We make no distinction between any of them, and unto Him we have surrendered' (Surah 2:136).

By then, other people had started coming in for the late evening prayer, so the Imam asked for us to continue the meeting at another time. Some people were upset about the lenient attitude of the Imam. Others were upset that I had been allowed to come into the mosque at all. Others thought that perhaps the Imam did not have knowledge, or did not want to entangle himself in the politics of it. Yet I could see a strange but hopeful look on some faces.

Atif asked me if he could accompany me to the bus stop since he was also going there. He was so joyous and happy. He wanted to hear more and ask more searching questions. As the next day we were off from work, we decided to meet each other at the gate of the central library for further discussion. When my bus arrived, he had graciously said, 'May God bless you and keep you safe' as I left.

Beside me on the chair was the Bible, the one I had given Atif the following day in the park, when we had sat for several hours and talked about Jesus and his mission. Since I had not yet given my response to the Imam's claim about the coming of Jesus as a follower of Muhammad, Atif had been curious to know what I thought of it. He had asked me if I would respond. I agreed to do so and was glad to have had some time to look into the subject again before meeting him the next day.

So, on the following day, I met Atif at our designated place. After tea and cake at a nearby restaurant, we went to a beautiful park nearby and found a quiet place to talk. We avoided the heat of the burning sun in the shade of the palm trees. I looked around and saw that there were a few people here and there, sitting, chatting to each other. A few were busy reading the daily newspapers. In one corner two gardeners were clearing the rubbish to prepare the ground for some flowers. A few yards away, a plumber was trying to clear a blockage to the fountain. In no time the fountain startd to flow again. 'Oh what scenery!' I exclaimed and Atif heard me. 'Yes!' he said. He was also looking around.

I was perturbed by the sound of a pair of crows who were attempting to destroy a sparrow's nest, but otherwise it was all calm. Content in spirit and relaxed in body, I was trying to fathom the majesty of God. I said to Atif, 'Isn't God sublime?'

'Surely he is, the *Rahman* and *Rahim*, the merciful, the Beneficent.'

I continued, 'God is dear. He is love, the lover and the beloved. He is great; see his greatness in the way that he is not negligent or careless toward anyone. He

nourishes the birds of the sky, the little animals on the
ground – even the humble ant which lives in the dirt. In
fact, the Bible states that he sends his sun and rains
both on the righteous and unrighteous.'

'Oh! It will be nice to have a copy of the Bible', he
said.

I took the copy I had intended to give him. 'Here it
is, a copy for you to keep and read.' He looked at me
with surprise and with much joy, and said, 'Thank
you.'

He was browsing through while I watched. Very
soon he was so drawn towards it that I had to deliberately make it obvious that I was still there. He apologised and said, 'Oh yes, we are here to discuss the rest
of what happened last night at the mosque.'

I smiled at his construction of phrases. He was quite
surprised when I told him that both Islam and Christianity share the belief that one day Jesus will return to
this earth. Atif knew that among Muslims this event is
known as *Nuzul-i-Isa*, the descent of Jesus. He seemed
to have had some idea from the popular Muslim traditions which say that when Jesus comes back, he will
convert the world to Islam, destroy the Antichrist,
marry and have children. Later he will die and be buried in a grave next to Muhammad in Madina.

Though there are many narrations of Jesus' coming
in the traditions of Islam, the Qur'an – which is the
first-hand authority for Muslims – has only one verse
to this effect. Hearing this, Atif was not sure, so I
opened my small copy of the Qur'an and showed him
the verse:

And lo! verily there is knowledge of the Hour. So doubt

ye not concerning it but follow Me. This is the right way (Surah 43:61).

He looked at the text in Arabic and then looked at its Urdu translation, 'but it is not clear whether it is talking about Jesus or something else', he complained.

'Yes! You are right', I replied, 'however, many Muslim scholars believe that it should be read as, "Jesus shall be a sign for the coming of the hour of Judgement." '

I shared with him the biblical narrative. He was surprised to find a major part of the New Testament directly concerned with Christ's second coming. I told him that, nevertheless, there was no mention of Jesus coming as an ordinary being, nor did the Bible give any suggestion of him coming to marry and then die some time later. He was now listening attentively. His interest in the subject encouraged me to continue.

'The Christian scriptures indicate that when Jesus comes, his people (both living and the dead) will be raised or changed to meet him in the air and the earth will be destroyed' (1 Corinthians 15:50–54; 1 Thessalonians 4:15–17; 2 Peter 3:10).

I shared with him that on many occasions Jesus said that he came from heaven, and that he would come again (John 3:13; 14:2–3,18–19; Matthew 25:31–32; 26:64). Though the first time he arrived as a baby, his second coming will be as the Mighty Judge and conquering King (2 Thessalonians 1:6–10). In the last chapter of the Bible, we find Jesus giving this reassuring news:

Behold, I am coming soon! My reward is with me, and I

will give to everyone according to what he has done (Revelation 22:12).

Atif interrupted, 'I was reading something the other day that in America some people believed they were themselves the second coming of Jesus.'

'Yes, there have been such people not only in the West but also in the East who have made such claims', I replied. 'Some groups like the Ahmadiyya and the Bahai believe that each of their founders was Jesus having come the second time. Other groups, like the Jehovah's Witnesses, believe that Jesus came back at the turn of this century, and that he took the chosen ones with him.'

'So, what do you think?' he asked quickly, looking anxious.

The sun was by now shining directly on us. Before going into further detail, we moved to another bench that lay under the thick shadow of a large tree. Atif was still looking eagerly at me waiting for my response. I looked at him and said, 'The Bible reveals that his second coming will not be a secret one. Neither will it be like his first coming, to be born again into this world.'

'Oh, so his descent will be the same as that which Muslims believe?' he asked.

Without answering his question, I said that while Jesus was ascending into heaven, the angels told his companions who were standing there watching him:

This same Jesus, who has been taken from you into heaven, will come back in the same way you have seen him go into heaven (Acts 1:11).

Muslim friends have various ideas. Some say that

Jesus will land on the minaret of the Umayyad mosque in Damascus, from where he will climb down by a ladder provided by the people within the mosque. Others claim he will land on the Ka'ba in Makkah, while yet others say he will descend in Jerusalem. However the place should not be in question; one has to think carefully that if he is coming from heaven, then this coming will not be an ordinary one, and with an ordinary body like ours. The Bible declares, in fact, that he is coming in heavenly splendour (2 Thessalonians 1:7) and his coming will be visible to everyone and will be so dramatic that no one will fail to recognise him (Matthew 24:30; Acts 1:9,11).

Unusually, an ice-cream vendor passed, so we bought some. It was certainly nice, and cooled us down. The ice-cream man was telling us he did not do much business, but perhaps in the evening when people came to the park with their children, he would be able to earn some more money. When Atif pointed out to him that the signboard in the park said no vendors allowed, he responded by saying, 'The very people who have put that sign are the ones who encouraged us to come in and sell, so that we can give them some pocket money'. and added, apologetically, 'You know what I mean.'

He stayed around us for a while and then moved on to someone else a hundred yards away, to sell his ice-cream. Atif did not hesitate to ask me, 'So, tell me more about the time and purpose of his coming in the light of the Bible. This is very interesting.'

'In the light of the Bible, as I see it', I said, opening the Bible, 'at his first coming Jesus became like us in every respect, to deliver us from the power of Satan. He came

to conquer sin and rise from the dead to gain victory
and triumph. At his second coming, we are going to see
him as he really is (John 1:18; Hebrews 2:14–17; 1 John
3:2). The proclamation of his gospel to the world will
cease when he comes. The doors of repentance will
close. Jesus, as a mighty Judge, will uproot all evil and
establish an eternal peace.'

'How will he do it?' Atif asked.

'Well, there are different interpretations but it
should not take us away from realising the awfulness
of that time, and the result of our belief and doings.'

'So, when will it be?' he asked. 'Can it be today, in a
year or two or as some Muslims say at the end of the
Islamic century?'

I assured him that the Bible speaks of his unexpected
return (Mark 13:32). 'We do not have to know about the
time, but we must be ready, and prepared for his
return at any time. Jesus said that his coming would be
as unexpected as the flood in the time of Noah (Matthew 24:37–41).'

I looked at Atif and said, 'Today, everyone has the
opportunity to believe in Christ and his message of salvation, now and as he commanded. At his arrival, this
chance will be withdrawn; it will then be too late.'

'Well, I do believe that Jesus is the chosen apostle of
God but as a Muslim I believe that it is not Jesus but
Muhammad (peace be upon him) whose message of
salvation is the final one. You see, I am told that
Prophets like Moses and Jesus prophesied the coming
of our Prophet and so I'm still not sure but, since I now
have the Bible, I will certainly study it.'

I assured him we could look into these matters again
but, to finish the conversation, I opened his copy of the

Bible and read to him:

> In the past God spoke to our forefathers through the prophets at many times and in various ways, but in these last days he has spoken to us by His Son, whom he appointed heir of all things, and through whom he made the universe (Hebrews 1:1–2).

Although I was at home resting, my mind and heart were still not at rest. Past memories continued flooding in until I was awoken by crying and lamenting in the street. Dragging my feet into a pair of broken *chappal* (slippers), I rushed to the door to see what had happened. The crying was from the house opposite. On the opposite side of the street, my neighbour's wife had just died during childbirth. Her husband was standing outside with his brothers while the women were shouting and crying inside.

After a while the midwife brought a little baby girl to him but he refused to take her in his arms.

'My wife died because of her. She is an omen of bad luck. She is evil', he shouted.

Finally, his brother took the baby while the other people there started to calm him down. I offered them the chance to sit in my house but they did not seem particularly interested.

'You are a Christian', my next-door neighbour and landlord said quietly. 'Go back to your house! Let them sort out their problem. They may treat your presence as unlucky and devilish.'

I was saddened by his remarks, and tiptoed back into the house. The sound of mourning and cries died down after an hour or two, but by then I was still tossing and turning in my bed. I was upset by their superstitious practices, thinking about that child who, if she lived, would grow up as an orphan in a society of superstition, a society where she will always be treated as the cause of any misfortune that occurred in that family for the rest of her life. She would be an outcast.

'*Allahu Akbar, Allahu Akbar.*' (Allah is the greatest, Allah is the greatest.) The call of morning prayer from the local mosque on the high pitch loudspeaker was a clear sign for me that another day was to begin. I just cried to the Lord, 'Give me more courage and a bit more of your peace.'

8

The Promised One

Though I had slept for only an hour when I got up, I felt calm and fresh. Another day was before me. As advised by my supervisor, I arrived in the office a few minutes earlier then usual to be called in by the Superintendent. A whole hour passed, but every time I asked his secretary, the Stenographer, he said, 'The boss is in the meeting, wait there.' After three hours waiting he told me that *Sab* (the boss) would like to see me in the afternoon.

'But my job? I am working, aren't I? I am to continue working, aren't I?' I asked him.

'I don't know.' He pretended to be ignorant and said, 'You have to check that with your supervisor.'

I took the stairs and went to the work floor to see my supervisor.

'What have you brought for me?' he asked, expecting some written note from the hierarchy. Finding none, he refused to sign me in and asked me to go back to get a note for permission to work.

No one was interested and I had to wait further for the Superintendent to see me. An hour before the office was to close, the secretary told me that *Sab* would like to see me tomorrow. I was tired, thirsty, hungry and upset within myself. Dismayed and distraught, I left the building.

'Lord!' I cried, 'Why? Why?'

In blind desperation and unaware of my surroundings I bumped into a bicycle. 'You want to die? Then find a bus or something else!' The cyclist waved his hand and shouted at me.

'*Mafi chahta hun*', (Forgive me) I said and without hearing any response, I kept walking.

After a while I was able to calm down, hoping for a better day tomorrow. Walking without any sense or purpose, I found myself in a market where the sale of animals, goats, sheep, cows and others was still continuing. Some were buying goats and sheep for their religious festival, *Eid al Adha*, for sacrifice. Muslims celebrate this feast to remember the sacrifice that Abraham offered. They recall that God put Abraham to the test by asking him to sacrifice his son and that at the right moment, God provided a ram in a thicket nearby, already prepared by God for that very moment. The Qur'an recounts this Biblical event in its own narrative style and states that it was a test of Abraham, and that God ransomed him with a tremendous sacrifice, 'Lo! that verily was a clear test. Then We ransomed him with a tremendous victim' (Surah 37:106–107).

The odour of *pakora* and *samosas* from the nearby vendor reminded me that I had not eaten my lunch. On the side of his stall, the vendor had put some benches and small tables. I was glad to have found such a cheap place. Thoughts of fear and hopelessness surrounded me as I asked myself if I had sufficient money to survive on if I lost my job, but I quickly ignored such feelings and thanked God for the present providence.

After that, I made my way back toward the bus stop to start my journey home. Someone also had a sheep on the bus. It was a typical picture of the buses which run between villages and small towns, loaded high with cattle and people all together. I soon realised from the conversation of the bus driver that the sheep was his.

I asked myself, 'Does this driver know why God prepared a ram to redeem Abraham's son?' I thought about the people who were travelling back to their home and families with lambs and goats and other animals for the *Eid* sacrifice. I asked myself, 'Do they know why God said, "We ransomed Abraham with a tremendous Sacrifice" and what that great sacrifice was?'

It is usual for Muslim commentators to say that the great sacrifice was the ram provided by God in place of Abraham's son. My friend Atif had put the same connotation on the story when I had asked him, 'Would a ram be a great sacrifice when compared with Abraham's son?'

He quickly saw the flaw in his thinking. He understood that it was not in the realm of reason to substitute a human being with an insignificant ram. When we study the event in biblical terms we find that as *Khalilullah*, the friend of God, Abraham understood that the ram was merely a symbol, a surety or pledge for the truly great sacrifice which God himself was to offer for redeeming Abraham, his son, his descendants and many others. Looking through the eyes of faith, he saw the great victim, the one who was going to be sacrificed for him and his prosperity.

'So what do you think! What sacrifice was it?' Atif was impatient with me. He said, 'As far as I know, the

Qur'an does not say anything further.'

I told him how the Bible records in great detail the background to Abraham's test and what the tremendous sacrifice was, the sacrifice by which God has ransomed Abraham but also all the faithful like him. The Bible confirms that God's Messiah, Jesus the Christ, is the one who has been made the sacrifice and ransom for the whole world.

John the Baptist who is known as *Yahya* among Muslims, said of Jesus, 'Look, the Lamb of God, who takes away the sin of the world!' (John 1:9). John gave Jesus this title to emphasise his role as a sacrifice, like the original lamb, but of much greater worth. Even Jesus testified about himself, 'Abraham rejoiced at the thought of seeing my day; he saw it and was glad' (John 8:56).

Explaining the purpose of his coming, Jesus reminded his audience again and again that he 'did not come to be served, but to serve, and to give his life as a ransom for many' (Matthew 20:28). By investigating both the New Testament and the Old Testament passages we can clearly conclude that Jesus is that great sacrifice. After his crucifixion, death, burial and resurrection, and when Jesus appeared among his companions, he explained his situation further to them and reminded them of the things that he had said to them:

This is what I told you while I was still with you: Everything must be fulfilled that is written about me in the Law of Moses, the Prophets and the Psalms. (Luke 24:44) ... This is what is written: The Christ will suffer and rise from the dead on the third day, and repentance and forgiveness of sins will be preached in his name to all nations, beginning at Jerusalem (Luke 24:46–47).

In response to their Master's instructions, his companions and other disciples took his message to the whole world, preaching him as the tremendous sacrifice provided by God himself as our ransom.

Amid these thoughts, I realised that the poor animal on the bus had done a 'wee' and it made a respectable-looking man of middle age very angry. He was on the way to a mosque somewhere nearby for a special evening meeting *Jalsah*. Now he had to do all the ritual washing and cleansing of his clothes once again. His dilemma was how to find the time to go back and change his clothes or to wash his clothes at the facilities of the mosque. He was beside himself.

Looking at him, I just quietly said, 'Is it not written somewhere, "*Al-amal bin niah*" (Man's action depends on his heart)? I am sure God knows your dilemma.'

He looked at me with a scowl and, without saying anything, walked towards the door at the back of the bus. I saw him leaving at the next stop, still examining his clothes.

When I reached home, I saw a few men sitting on *charpai* outside the deceased woman's home. After a short time of greetings and condolences, I entered my home to find out that my landlord had used all the water and had connected some wires to the electricity line so that the grieving household would have some light instead of kerosene lamps. I thanked God that people still cared for neighbours.

And that night, though I myself was in a kind of turmoil, I realised that I was praying for the newly born child in the house opposite, for her father and her extended family. There was a lot to pray about: for myself, about what was happening around me and about a community where people wished to have male children, a community where female children were treated as a liability; where many prayers were said for the gift of sons; few were said for the daughters.

I was so tired that I fell asleep only to be awoken by the voice of the *muezzin* from the local mosque on the loud speaker early the next morning. It was also a joy to hear the sound of water in the cemented water tank again. At least I could wash properly. With these necessary amenities, I was able to make myself a cup of tea and to consume it with some sweetbread.

That morning was no different from others. The same sun arose from the eastern horizon and an hour later was blazing on the faces of us all as we waited in the queue. A bus arrived and everybody rushed towards it as usual, not bothering to queue. Everybody was trying to get on the bus. Once again it was going to be hopeless if another bus did not arrive. With much so-called 'luck' I got on to the following bus with one thing on my mind: not to lose my humanity, no matter what happened in the office that day.

I was half an hour early. As soon as the office opened, I went to the waiting area outside the Superintendent's office. I thought the secretary would be surprised to see me at such an early time. He wasn't. An hour later the Superintendent arrived with his porter carrying his briefcase. He looked at me and without saying anything turned to his secretary. I stood up politely, ready to be summoned, but he did not. Instead he went straight into his office.

While sitting there, I thought about how much

things had changed. It was in that very office that the same high officer had himself filled in my application form all those years ago and had made sure that I got the job and was sent for training. He did this because the head of the family that cared for me was his friend.

Things had drastically changed. Now I had no support from that family, all because of my change of views about life and change of faith. I waited and waited. At last, the stenographer came with a piece of paper for me. I was suspended because of my leave of absence without advance agreement, and because of my irresponsible, irregular and improper sorting of mail, and my wasting of office time over tea when holding sectarian discussions. According to the charge sheet that I was given three days later, I had to appear before a sub-committee to decide whether or not I was to be dismissed from service. With a heavy heart, I went to the payroll office to collect my salary, and check if there was something for me in the post.

I was back at the bus stop by noon and ready to return home. It was the same bus stop where Atif and I used to chat and share ideas while waiting for a bus. At this time of the day one does not have to wait for a bus very long. A bus going to my destination was still waiting for the passengers. I was able to get a seat near the window. After a few minutes, we were moving. A great throng of people were on the streets; shops were open and the displays were inviting anyone to come in and buy.

After a mile, there was a bang and a terrible noise came from under the bus. The bus swerved but somehow stopped. The driver calmly but quickly announced to us, 'The axle is broken. I will refund your tickets so you can get another bus.'

Like others I got a refund for my ticket and made my
way to the nearest bus stop. While waiting for that bus,
I looked in front of me. Opposite me was the restaurant
where Atif and I used to come to celebrate pay day.
Without thinking, I crossed the road and entered the
restaurant. It was a little more than a month ago since
we had spent an evening together there. I asked the
receptionist and waiter if I could sit at the table where
we used to sit. They gladly let me. Nothing seemed to
have changed – it was I who had changed. I had lost a
friend. And now I was about to lose my job. A waiter
came and left the menu. What could I order? Somehow
my appetite had disappeared.

I asked for some tea and snacks. Atif and I used to sit
in front of each other, in order to talk more comfortably, face to face. The sofa-type seat on the other side of
the table where he sat last time was now empty. It was
here that we would spend at least two to three hours at
one sitting. After a meal we used to sip tea and, to keep
the manager happy, we used to order every half hour
more tea so that we could to get on with our discussion.

Though Atif was already becoming convinced about
the uniqueness of Jesus, he was still looking to see if
there was a ray of hope somewhere in the pages of the
Torah and the Injil which would let him continue to
believe in the faith in which he was born and brought
up. He had studied hard, so I was glad that he used to
give me ample time in advance to discuss an issue he
thought was very important to him.

It was in this restaurant that he had asked me for my
comments on the prophecies about the Prophet of
Islam in the Torah and the Injil. The Qur'an seems to

claim that a prophet like Muhammad was mentioned in the Torah, and so Muslim friends feel obliged to find passages which will fit him and his mission.

The most prominent among these is the passage where we find Moses saying to the Israelites, 'God will raise up for you a prophet like me from among your own brothers. You must listen to him.' He told them further, 'The LORD said to me: "...I will raise up for them a prophet like you from among their brothers; I will put my words in his mouth, and he will tell them everything I command him. If anyone does not listen to my words that the prophet speaks in my name, I myself will call him to account."' (Deuteronomy 18:15–18)

I remembered, one evening, Atif read to me some comments from Muslim writers saying that the word 'brothers' in this passage referred to another nation – that is, the Arabs – among whom Muhammad rose as the prophet. As Moses brought a book for the people, so Muhammad came with a book. And as Moses fought with enemies, so did Muhammad. Similarly, as Moses married and had a family, so did Muhammad.

Atif was anxious to hear my response. He was uneasy as he saw that I was silent for a while. Before he could say anything, though, I responded that most of the comparative examples he gave me could fit anybody claiming to be a prophet. It could fit even *Musailmah*, who claimed prophethood in the last days of Muhammad with a book like the Qur'an. The comparative picture that is painted by several Muslims may fit most of the prophets that were born from the time of Moses until the time of Jesus.

'However let's go back to the beginning of this whole

issue', I said as I opened my Bible. He smiled, knowing that I was going to say as I had during previous discussions, that we should always look at the text and its context. As the Qur'an is taken to be its own exposition, the same applies to the Bible. As usual, he was in full attention.

Starting with the key word 'brothers' in the passage, I told him that it did not refer to another nation but Israel.

'Is that so? How?' Again he was quick to interrupt. I calmed him down and started to reiterate that even if we left the whole of the Torah on one side and just looked in Deuteronomy from where the passage came, we would be able to remove any misunderstanding.

'In this part of the Torah', I told him, 'the word *brothers* is used about 48 times and not once was it used for Ishmailites or Arabs.'

'Let me give you some examples,' I said and quoted the first two verses of the same chapter where the prophecy is usually thought to be about Muhammad:

> The priests, who are Levites – indeed the whole tribe of Levi – are to have no allotment or inheritance with *Israel* … They shall have no inheritance among their *brothers*; the Lord is their inheritance, as he promised them (Deuteronomy 18:1–2).

I shared with him that this passage taught that the Levites were a tribe of Israel and the word 'brothers' mentioned in verse 2 referred to the other eleven tribes of Israel.

Just one chapter before this passage we find that God instructed Moses to advise the Israelites how to choose a king. He told them:

Be sure to appoint over you the king the LORD your
God chooses. He must be from among your own brothers (Deuteronomy 17:15).

There is no mention in this passage about the children of Ishmael as brothers of the tribes of Israel. The
Israelites always chose kings from among their own
twelve tribes.

I added, 'If it was not meant to be the case, then those
prophets among them who followed one after another
would have told them to give a chance to the
Ishmailites as well. Their silence on this matter is evidence that the word *brothers* in this context only meant
the Israelites. In the light of this, we may understand
that when the promise of the Prophet was given, the
Israelites understood that he was to be from among
them – an Israelite – and was to be their brother.'

Though Atif was studying the Bible, he still pre-
ferred the Qur'anic evidence. In this case I could provide him with some examples from the Qur'an, so I
continued, saying that a prophet was a brother of those
among whom he was born and to whom he was sent.
We can find other examples of this in the Qur'an. A
prophet *Hud* is called the brother of the tribe *A'd* (Surah
7:65). Similarly, we find the same concerning the
prophets, *Salih* and *Shuaib* (Surah 7:73,85). Thus when
Moses was given the good news of the coming
prophet, it was understood that he was to rise from
among the Israelites.

Sitting there at the table I remembered how impatient he used to be. Often, I had to calm him. He was a
little surprised when I mentioned to him that according to the Torah (Deuteronomy 34:1–21) for the one like

Moses there would be two prominent signs: (1) God should speak to him directly; (2) he should be a mighty miracle worker.

I showed Atif from the Bible how we learn that God spoke to Moses face to face and gave him his commandments directly (Exodus 33:11). Muslims recognise this attribute and call him 'Kalim-u-llah' (he with whom God conversed). However, the Qur'an suggests that God sent his words to Muhammad through the angelic intermediary, Gabriel, and through other means (Surah 2:97). By contrast, we see that not only did God speak to Jesus but that he himself is his Word (John 1:1; Surah 3:35). The fist sign is therefore fulfilled in Jesus.

The second sign of this coming prophet was that he was to be a mighty sign and miracle worker. Atif was already acquainted with the miracles mentioned in the Gospels that Jesus performed. We find evidence in the Qur'an that Jesus performed unique miracles (Surah 5:110,111,113; 19:21). I told him that I found in the Qur'an that Muhammad was not granted such a facility (Surah 29:50).

Atif was listening very carefully, which gave me a further chance to continue. To support my point of view, I quoted from the New Testament section of the Bible by mentioning to him that when Jesus spoke and people witnessed his signs and wonders, they proclaimed:

> We have found the one Moses wrote about in the Law, and about whom the prophets also wrote (John 1:45). Surely this is the Prophet who is to come into the world (John 6:14).

I shared with him how the apostles of Jesus proclaimed that Jesus had fulfilled the prophecy given through Moses (Acts 3:11–26; 7:37–60). Jesus also claimed that Moses and other prophets wrote about his coming (Luke 24:44). He said to some unbelieving Jews of his time the clear words, 'If you believed Moses, you would believe me, for he wrote about me'' (John 5:46).

In fact, Jesus said in very open words to his audience, 'If you do not believe that I am the one I claim to be, you will indeed die in your sins' (John 8:24; cf. Deuteronomy 18:19).

I remembered we were both silent for a while. At last he said, 'I seem to be in trouble here and in need of lots of prayers and support.'

I assured him of my prayers, and quoted what Jesus said:

> Ask and it will be given to you; seek and you will find; knock and the door will be opened to you. For everyone who asks receives; he who seeks finds; and to him who knocks, the door will be opened (Matthew 7:7–8).

'Are you all right sir?' I was startled by the waiter's voice. 'Oh, I am sorry.' Yes, Yes, I am fine', I replied. While deep in thought, I had not noticed him bringing my tea and it was now cold. Still I drank some and, after paying the bill, I left. I was feeling embarrassed and promised myself not to lose myself in a daydream again.

9

The Advocate

I lived in an area where people always tried to find out what others were doing. To know who was coming and who was leaving was their second nature. So it was not unusual that my neighbour was a little surprised when he saw me appearing in the street unusually early. I greeted him as normally as I could. To share what had happened in the office would not have been good. He could have told my landlord, who would have been concerned for his rent, and would have started asking me to vacate the house. I was therefore reluctant to face such a fiasco in a society where it is not easy for a bachelor to find a room let alone a house to rent. Families are suspicious of such bachelors living alone in their streets, afraid of their motives, thinking perhaps that they just want to corrupt local girls.

I had bought some vegetables and other groceries from a shop at the bus stop near my home, so I spent most of the evening cooking. Cooking at home for one person was expensive in Pakistan at that time. I could eat more cheaply at a nearby café. Accordingly, cooking was something I never liked, but it was a good excuse to occupy myself. After some struggle, what I prepared looked nice on the table. Very soon, the salty and burnt taste of the vegetables overcame my hunger. I was glad that I had not invited anyone to dinner. I usually took my guest to a restaurant or bought some cooked food, such as a take-away, beforehand.

When I washed the few utensils and cleaned the little kitchen – after getting rid of a few cockroaches – I was ready to sit and relax. The sea breeze seemed refreshing. I pulled out some of my course books to see if I could return to studying. My dream was to get a degree in Islamic studies. In fact Atif had joined me in this aim, although his subjects were mainly related to Islamic history, and not theology. I thought it would have been nice to have had fellowship, but God had had a different purpose.

After spending some time in reading one of the course books, I switched on the radio. As usual, it was tuned to a Christian radio station in the Seychelles. Even though I could hear and make sense of what I heard, here and there the sound used to disappear for a few seconds. It was a Bible study programme and the subject was the Holy Spirit. I put aside my course book and reached for the Bible and started following what the presenter was saying. I soon realised that I had only caught up with the study towards the end of it. After that there were some Christian hymns and songs in the Urdu language which I liked very much. Sadly, I come from a family who treated music and songs as satanic art. Indeed, once my father heard me singing among friends and there and then beat me so hard that I never dared to sing again.

More than singing, I was still thinking about the Bible study on the Holy Spirit. As a Muslim, it was a

subject I did not know much about. Though the word
for spirit, *ruh*, is used twenty-one times in the Qur'an,
nowhere is it used so clearly as in the Bible and especially in the New Testament. In fact, when people
asked Muhammad about the definition and the working of it, the only revelation he claimed to have
received is: 'They will question thee concerning the
Spirit. Say: The Spirit is by command of my Lord, and
of knowledge ye have been vouchsafed but little'
(Surah 17:85).

The Qur'an speaks of the Holy Spirit, *Ruh al-Quds*,
also but Muslims take it to be the title of the angel
Gabriel. Yet the Holy Spirit, as mentioned as the comforter in the New Testament, is interpreted by them to
be Muhammad.

Muslims refer to some of the passages in the Gospel
according to John and play on the Greek word
Paraclete, which is translated as Helper, Comforter,
Counsellor and Advocate in English translations of the
Bible:

> And I will ask the Father, and he will give you another
> Counsellor to be with you for ever – the Spirit of truth.
> (John 14:16) But the Counsellor, the Holy Spirit, whom
> the Father will send in my name, will teach you all
> things and will remind you of every thing I have said to
> you (John 14:26).

My friend Atif was no different in this case. He in line
with other Muslims thought that these verses surely
referred to the coming of Muhammad. As on other
occasions, he asked me how I disagreed with the
Islamic view. He even gave me a booklet printed
by the *Jamiat Talaba*, the Students Union at Karachi

University.

I reminded myself how I had shared with him a sound exegesis of the passages and their context (John, chapters 14 to 16), in which we find that the verses about the Paraclete cannot be a prophecy about Muhammad for the following reasons:

1. The passage of John which Muslims quote to us is, 'He will give you another *Helper* (or, as Muslims believe, Muhammad) to be with you forever' (John 14:17). This passage becomes clear when we read it with another passage in which Jesus tells his disciples, 'I have much more to say to you, more than you can now bear. But when he, the Spirit of truth, comes, he will guide you into all the truth' (John 16:12–13). In other words Jesus says, 'I have been your counsellor, Comforter, your *Paraclete*. I have many things to say to you but I send to you the Spirit of truth, *another* Counsellor, *another* Helper, *another* Paraclete.' Another passage declares Jesus as our advocate, *Paraclete* with the Father (1 John 2:1) and it was in this sense that he promised to give his disciples another Paraclete. So one of the major roles of the Holy Spirit is to be pleader, intercessor and our advocate. In Arabic for such the word *Wakil* is used. However, in the Qur'an, Muhammad has not been given such title nor the authority by God. Very often he was asked by God to tell people that he was not their *Wakil* (Surah 10:108; 17:54; 42:6).

2. This advocate, Comforter or Paraclete had to be here for ever, 'to be with you for ever'. Muhammad lived on this earth for about 63 years and then died.

3. Jesus also said, 'The Spirit of truth. The world cannot accept him, because it neither sees him nor knows him. But you know him, for he lives with you and will be in you' (John 14:17). The world could not see this Holy Spirit, the Comforter, or know him as he is an invisible purely spiritual being. Muhammad was seen both by his followers and opponents in his time. The Qur'an claims that Muhammad came for the whole world to accept him as a messenger of God (Surah 21:107; 25:1; 34:28).

4. No Muslims believe that Muhammad was sent in Jesus' name, yet the Holy Spirit, the counsellor, the advocate was to be sent by God in Jesus' name (John 14:26). Jesus said that the Spirit will *glorify* him (John 16:14). Instead of glorifying Jesus, Muhammad made himself as the seal of the prophets and the leader of them all, including Jesus. By doing so, he made Jesus an inferior prophet. The prime purpose of sending the *Paraclete* was to convict and draw people toward Jesus. He was not to speak of himself but of Jesus. Muhammad however drew people from Jesus to himself and thus he cannot be the promised *Paraclete*, the Comforter.

5. Jesus repeated his promise before his ascension. He told them to wait in Jerusalem until the Holy Spirit came and, some days later as the disciples were gathered praying, it happened as he promised (Acts 2:3–4). This promise was fulfilled several centuries before Muhammad was born (Acts 2:1–4, 33,38; 1 Corinthians 12:13; Ephesians 1:13,14; 5:18; Romans 8:9:11,13–16). The disciples at that moment knew

that the promise of the Holy Spirit, the counsellor and the comforter, was fulfilled. The Holy Spirit transformed them and gave them the indomitable courage to stand up and be counted on Jesus' side. From then on, they proclaimed publicly what they believed. The Holy Spirit gave them the willpower and a dynamism they had previously lacked to go forth to preach the risen Jesus: 'God has raised this Jesus to life, and we are all witness of the fact. Exalted to the right hand of God, he has received from the Father the promised Holy Spirit and has poured out what you now see and hear' (Acts 2:32–33).

I remembered how Atif had insisted that I give him these points in writing so that he could discuss them with some Muslim scholars. I gladly did and, several days later when I asked him about the outcome, he said that he was still looking into it.

In the midst of all these memories, I thanked the Lord for his helping hand to know the truth of Jesus. Somewhere, in the back of my mind, there was a desire to know 'what did Atif think about Jesus after all?' I went into the room and got out his Bible that his brother had returned to me. I checked the passages in which the promise of the Holy Spirit is mentioned and found a note written beside those verses on the margin, 'This promise was fulfilled in the very life of the disciples.'

I asked myself, 'Did he then believe in Jesus as the *rahmah*, mercy of God for all people of the earth?'

My thoughts were halted by the noise of knocking on the door. I went to look. There was a child with a bucket asking if I could give him some drinking water as their *matka*, big earthen storage jar had broken. I gladly filled the bucket and gave it to him. Minutes later there were two more children with buckets, asking if they could fill their buckets from the storage tank. After an hour the tank was empty and my landlord standing outside his gate was laughing at my foolishness in letting them take it all.

'The employees of the water board are going to be on strike for the next couple of days. There will be no water', he mocked. 'And I am not going to give you a drop of water, even if you are to die of thirst.'

I smiled: 'It is better for one to die so that many more may live.'

'Only God can understand your philosophy', he murmured, waving his hand in farewell.

Coming in the room, I suddenly realised the significance of what I had just said.

10

Words of Men

Early in the morning I was awoken by the sound of monsoon rain. As a result, though the water was murky, there was plenty of it. The strike did not take place after all. The rainwater from the courtyard had found its way in the sitting room. I removed the cheap *dari*, rug, from the cemented floor. The rain was over by afternoon. The air was clean and fresh. I went out to get some milk from the corner café. There were big puddles in the streets. Some kind-hearted people had laid some bricks and wooden planks so that people could cross over.

At the shop and café the radio with its amplifier was at full blast. Indian and Pakistani film songs with erotic words were an open violation of the code of an Islamic life and yet no one seemed to mind. While paying for the milk and tea bags pack, a familiar voice taunted me. '*Oye, choohra chamar too yahan rehta hai*' (O sweeper, you live around here)'.

I turned around to see that it was Farooq. He was one of the leaders of the extremist Islamic group at the university campus and was a troublemaker. He and his two friends once beat me up just because I shared why I had accepted Jesus and become a Christian and did not remain a Muslim.

To stay there further was to invite trouble. I said nothing, paid my bill and walked away. I quietly pleaded with God, 'Please, Lord, help me.'

On reaching my house door, I looked back and was happy to see that Farooq had not followed me.

I thanked God for not letting him make a spectacle. However, his calling me *choohra chamar* had alerted the shopkeeper. Though the term is used in Hinduism for someone from a low caste, Muslims in poor areas use this term for Christians, especially for those who earn their living by sweeping streets and taking the rubbish away to tips. Many Muslims would not allow such people to eat in a restaurant or use others' utensils. Thus in small towns they must carry their own utensils to get food, water or tea to take away. In cities such a practice is not practicable but in villages and towns the custom carries on and they are treated as social lepers.

At the campus, Farooq had influential backing. He was so successful that he even managed to uproot and force some peaceful lecturers away from the university just because, in his opinion, they were too liberal in their Islamic belief. From time to time he used to distribute Islamic literature in English and Urdu.

Once he distributed more than a thousand copies of a pseudo Gospel of Barnabas in English and Urdu, claiming it to be the real, original gospel of Jesus. I had bought copies of it in Urdu and English a year before and had studied the responses of Christian scholars to it, and shared with several students that the so-called gospel of Barnabas was a forgery.

Atif one day invited some students to listen to me explain why I thought Muslims should not have published the book because it was also against the teaching of the Qur'an. About fifteen of us gathered in the common room.

I went into the introduction of how the so-called book was found and how it appeared in its present form but most of the students were not interested. One student sitting in the front waved a copy of the gospel of Barnabas at me shouting, 'We heard you say that this book is anti-Qur'an. Tell us how!'

Another beside him raised his voice, 'If you don't, then you are a liar.'

'He already is a liar, *Kafir, Murtad* (unbeliever, apostate)' someone commented.

'Right!' I raised my voice in reply. 'Let me come straight to it then.' I opened my notebook. Atif pleaded with everyone to calm down and listen. Somehow all went quiet. Thanking them, I started by referring to how at the campus copies of the so-called Gospel of Barnabas were distributed by a group of students calling it the '*Asli Injil*' (the original gospel) which is mentioned in the Qur'an.

I stated what scholars had found; that the real Barnabas would not have made certain geographical and historical mistakes which are found in this gospel. They are certain that this gospel is a late medieval forgery. However, that is not all.

Some students at the campus had been arguing that this gospel is in harmony with the Qur'an in its teaching about the crucifixion of Jesus and several other matters. Therefore they claimed that it must be the same gospel the Qur'an talks about.

I put forward the Christian case that although the Qur'an and this gospel shared the same theology concerning the crucifixion, there was very little else upon which their teaching coincided. For example, Muslims believe that the original 'Gospel' must have descended upon Jesus. However, this gospel has a Christian understanding of inspiration rather than the Muslim concept.

This document mentions Jesus reciting the Muslim creed (*Shahada*), 'There is no God but Allah and Muhammad is his prophet.' However, this creed was not laid down until 600 years after Jesus and even in the Qur'an it is never given as one complete statement at one time.

I continued, 'The Qur'an accepts Jesus as the Messiah but the Jesus in this gospel refuses to accept the title' (Chapter 42). Instead Muhammad is mentioned as the Messiah. Nowhere does the Qur'an describe Muhammad as *al-Masih*.

'This gospel portrays Mary as giving birth to Jesus without pain (Chapter 3). It also claims that Jesus' birth took place in a shepherd's house or shelter. In contrast to this the Qur'an vividly relates the pangs of childbirth, which drove Mary to cry out in pain, and asserts that Jesus was born under a palm tree in the wilderness while no one else was present except him and his mother.

'According to this gospel, there are nine heavens and ten hells (Chapters 52, 57, 178), but the Qur'an teaches only seven heavens (Surah 2:29). This gospel teaches that Satan is the creator of hell (Chapter 135), whereas the Qur'an teaches that God is the creator of hell (Surah 25:11).

'In this gospel, we are told that before the last day comes, there will be a fifteen-day schedule of step-by-step destruction (Chapter 53). It further states that on the thirteenth day the heavens shall be rolled up like a book and every living thing shall die. All this is in clear contradiction with the Qur'an which states that men will be alive until the last day (Surah 80:33–37). The Qur'an nowhere mentions the death of the holy angels, but asserts that they will still perform their duty (Surah 69:15–17).

'This gospel states that the Tawrat became contaminated, so God sent another book, the Zabur or Psalms. When this in turn was altered, God gave the Injil – the Gospel. This theory holds that when a divine book is altered, God sends another book. Consequently, when the Gospel was altered God sent the Qur'an. This raises an important question with regard to the Gospel of Barnabas. If, as many among you believe, this is the true and original Gospel, then in the light of such a theory there is no need for the Qur'an.'

I was just about to make a conclusion when Farooq and a few heavy-handed students burst into the room and threw a chair at me. Others joined him in kicking me. After a few blows on my head, I felt as though the walls were falling down at me. The shouting of Atif and others was fading and when I came to my senses I was lying under a tree. Atif and two other students helped me to sit up. My shirt was wet with blood and two students were trying to clean the wound on my forehead.

The department head was very unhappy about the incident and blamed me for the excitement. Somehow the whole matter was dismissed as an unhappy accident simply to be brushed aside. Atif was feeling guilty as the discussion had been his idea. Though this incident had put me off my daily routine for a whole week, somehow it changed Atif's attitude and way of reasoning. He became more open to listening, to comparing, to reasoning and to concluding things for himself.

Farooq, along with his merry men, never liked me and always mocked me. They even scared the restaurant contractor at the campus by saying that, as I was now an unclean person, if they saw me eating or drinking at his shop, then they would not dine there themselves and would stop all other students as well. The restaurant owner soon asked me not to visit his shop again, in order to retain his business. Atif was very unhappy about such discrimination, but I gave in and agreed not to come to the canteen anymore.

I had already enough problems to deal with and now here I was to face the rumours of being a *Chohra*, unclean. I did not have to wait long. Just an hour later someone knocked on the door. Concerned at what had happened just a while ago, I was not sure whether to open the door. I tiptoed towards the door and peeped through the corner. Seeing a child with an empty cup in his hand, I sighed with relief and opened the door.

'Uncle! Please give us some sugar. Our ration is due next week, and I will return it then.'

'Let me check if there is some.' While he waited I went to the kitchen. I had enough and gave him a cup full.

He was very happy to see a full cup and thanked me while leaving. As I was about to close the door, one of his friends joined him. They both stopped. I could hear him saying, 'You should not have taken the sugar. He is *Chohra*, unclean.'

They walked away and I could not hear them any more. Closing the door I felt very unhappy. Going straight to the kitchen I made a cup of tea to pass the time until dinner in the evening. Tea with a few biscuits seemed a pleasant luxury. Most of that afternoon was spent listening to some tapes, songs and news. The news was not good. The political situation of the country was once again in upheaval. Though the regime had promised to pave the way for an election, the people on the street knew from past experience that such promises of *soon* change into months and years.

I still remember how like many young Muslims, Atif used to be an active member of *Jamat Islami*. He thought that by introducing Islamic rule in the country, all his and his countrymen's problems would be solved. His dream was shattered when he realised how various parties were buying and selling votes and loyalties. The whole election system seemed a charade. Even those who came to power by promising Islamic socialism did not succeed. In his opinion, it was important to first establish an Islamic government if people were to be changed and then follow true Islam – Islam as it should be.

The reading of some writings of the Indo-Pakistan scholar Mawdudi, and Qutb of *Ikhwan al-Muslimin* of Egypt, was very much in evidence in Atif's thinking. However, by reading the Christian scriptures, and analysing them, he soon realised that unless people themselves wholeheartedly accept what they believe in, no government and no law could make them assimilate it.

If people practise Islam because of the fear of an Islamic government, then it will amount to hypocrisy and certainly God does not like the hypocrites or their hypocrisy.

Atif's brother was different. He did not like Atif's fellowship with me but, because of his mother's openness, he had changed his hardness of heart. I was somewhat puzzled by his cold attitude and the way he had returned all that he found in Atif's locker as 'Christian material'. He must have thought that I had given it to him. Yet most of the material was not in fact mine. It was also obvious that Atif would not have kept all his books, other printed matter and tapes in his locker at work. Perhaps now as Atif was not among us, his brother did not want others to see the 'Christian stuff' lying around in the house and thus jeopardise their position in society.

Atif's mother was very different, an educated but very simple woman and open to discussion about Jesus. Though she had some peculiar ideas, she often confessed that the teaching and example of love and kindness displayed by Jesus was unique. By contrast with Muhammad, she could see in Jesus the miracle-performing prophet *par excellence*. His suffering, rather than 'Islamic-type triumphalism', was often appreciated by her. She was more like the Muslims from Sufi circles, who stressed the love of God and his relation with his people. Yet there were times when she would try to hide behind the facade of religious songs known as *Qawali* and would quote:

Khuda jo pakray choda lain Muhammad.
Muhammad jo pakray chora koi nahi sakta.

(When God convicts someone, Muhammad will intercede, but when Muhammad convicts someone, no one
can intercede.)

Qawali songs have very much influenced many
Indian Muslims. Some of these songs exalt Muhammad to the place of God. Often when a qawali reaches
its climax, it is said in a repeated refrain, 'If Muhammad had not been, God himself wouldn't have
existed.'

The Qur'an, the Muslim's firsthand authority, states
that Muhammad was just a prophet like all other
prophets, and he was sent to lead mankind towards the
straight path (Surah 3:144). To many Muslims, he is
Sarware Kayanat and *Sardare do Jahan* – Master of the
creation and master of the two worlds, but in the
Qur'an we find him saying, 'I cannot benefit even
myself' (Surah 7:188; 17:93; 46:9).

Atif's mother knew that the Qur'an does not exalt
Muhammad in a way that is found in the traditions of
Islam. It is only in the books of traditions that Muhammad is mentioned as having the gift of miracles, but in
the Qur'an we do not find that he had such a power. It
was more than a century later that stories of his per-
forming miracles began to grow. These included stories around his birth, his night ascension and the like,
yet the Qur'an shows clearly that he did not possess the
power of miracles (Surah 6:37, etc.).

Though Atif's mother disagreed with lot of things I
said, she was a very open-minded lady and always
tried to leave the discussion open for further debate.

11

Defeat or Victory

That evening, when I went to the corner café, the owner behaved as I had suspected. He quietly asked me not to eat at his café again, or even to come to it. I left and walked the mile to a different restaurant near the local cinema, avoiding the mud and puddles as I went. Sitting at the restaurant, I could see some of the billboards with pictures of adverts for various films. To fill the gap between Urdu films, the cinema was, like many others, showing an English film. Although most of the patrons could not understand the dialogue, they could at least follow the story.

I was surprised to see that it was showing *Ben Hur*, a film that had been banned a few years earlier; it had been shown in the main theatres for a few weeks. The censors withdrew it because the film shows the incident of crucifixion, which conflicts with Islamic belief. Muslims believe that Jesus was never crucified.

I saw that a crowd was coming out. The matinee show had just finished. A few of them entered the restaurant and sat for tea while some ordered meals. I was amazed to hear their comments.

'Oh, *yar*, it seemed real', one exclaimed sitting at the table beside mine.

Another said, 'I thought they were going to show his face but they didn't.'

'Did this really happen to *Hazrat Isa*?' One asked his friend.

Without really answering his question, his friend said, 'I wish they could show him going up into heaven.'

'Was Jesus really crucified?' He repeated his question again.

'Not really, it is just a story', said another of his friends as he cupped his hand, striking a match to light his cigarette despite the draughtt from the pedestal fan nearby.

'Well, Christians believe it happened', I butted in, 'but they also believe that on the third day Jesus rose victoriously.'

They all looked at me curiously. A very thin man with big focal glasses with a bag on his shoulder who was reading the small print of a thick paperback said, 'You must have read a lot about Christianity.'

'Not much, but so far what I have read has convinced me that though Jesus was crucified and died, he also rose and then ascended to heaven from where he will come back one day.'

'No, No, God does not allow his beloved holy prophets to die such a death.' The man waved his hands in the air saying, 'It will be an utter defeat. This will show that Jesus was a failure.'

His reaction reminded me of Peter when Jesus told him about his death and resurrection: his response was, 'Never, Lord! This shall never happen to you' (Matthew 16:22).

To respond to his Peter-like reaction, I said, 'Well,

that may be one view but the Qur'an states that God
has allowed his people to be killed. To follow the view
that Jesus dying on the cross is a failure is utterly
wrong because he overcame his death on the cross by
his becoming alive again to show that even death could
not hold him.'

I intended to continue but one of the waiters butted
in, 'No religious and political discussion here. Other
people are waiting. Let us do some business to provide
our children with some bread and water.'

After paying our bills we came out and I told the thin
man that if they wanted to continue the discussion, we
could do so, but his friends dragged him away. I felt so
sorry.

I took the road back to my dwelling in the dark of
that late evening. The yellowish light on some poles
proved to be landmarks which told me where the road
was leading to. The sky was full of stars. Here and
there, I would see a shooting star. My mind and heart
could not help but testify that all this did not happen
just by itself. There is a creator, I thought, who is the
God of us all. I just praised him for all that beauty, and
for everything.

'But, can he provide the solution to the present
dilemma that you are in?' one side of me asked.

'Yes, he will. In his own time, he will do what is best
for me.'

At home that night I opened the scriptures for my
daily reading as was my routine. The passage was:

For the message of the cross is foolishness to those who
are perishing, but to us who are being saved it is the
power of God (1 Corinthians 1:18).

After reading a few pages, I started to ponder on the things that had taken place that day. In my desperation I tried to look for the positive aspects in my life, times when God had been gracious to me. And then I came back to the theme of the passages that I had read. I thought about the traditional Islamic denial of the crucifixion of Jesus and about how I found that the opposite of it was more acceptable.

Like many others, Atif and his mother also objected to the idea of the crucifixion of Christ. Though Atif had studied the subject with me, he did not want to offend his mother, and let her ask me questions. I certainly will not forget the occasion when Atif invited me for dinner at his home. His brother was on some business in another city and thus we were only three at the table. It was a happy occasion. We had home-made food but, more importantly, we each shared and exchanged views. We talked about several things but each time the subject changed, we spoke about the person of Jesus. Atif's mother was at heart a devoted Muslim but was not prejudiced against other people's views. In contrast to many Muslims, she was sufficiently open to examine spiritual values with a critical understanding.

She knew that according to Christians and their scriptures, the plan of salvation and eternal life are connected with the crucifixion of Jesus, his death and his resurrection. No wonder then, that at the peak of our discussion she asked me, 'Masood! If, somehow, it could be proved that Jesus was not crucified, then what would be your reaction?'

Before I could reply Atif said, 'It will be the end of trustworthiness.'

'He is right, Auntie!' I said. 'If Jesus was not crucified

then it would mean that Christ was a deceiver, for he spoke about his death beforehand. He told his followers that he must go to Jerusalem and suffer many things at the hands of his enemies and be killed and raised again on the third day (Matthew 16:21). Jesus on several occasions said that he came to give his life as a ransom for many (Matthew 20:28).'

'But – but what about the Qur'an which says that Jesus was not crucified. What would you say to that?' she asked me. Atif also looked at me.

'As far as I know', I continued, 'in the Qur'an there is only one reference that doubts Jesus' crucifixion, but in the New Testament we have verse after verse saying that Jesus did die on the cross.'

'Masood!' she interrupted me. 'I would rather like to know how you managed to overcome the Qur'anic denial of crucifixion of Jesus.'

'Well, Brother, come on. Be open. She is not one of those who are afraid of the fragility of their faith', Atif encouraged me.

I collected my thoughts and began by saying, 'The Qur'an does indeed talk about the death of Jesus in several of its verses, but refers to the crucifixion only once and that verse can be interpreted as denying both the crucifixion of Jesus and his death on the cross at the hands of the Jews. The Qur'an points out that the Jews claimed, "We killed Christ Jesus, the son of Mary, the apostle of God; but they killed him not, nor crucified him, but so it was made to appear to them, and those who differ therein are full of doubt, with no (certain) knowledge, but only conjecture to follow, for of a surety they killed him not" (Surah 4:157).'

'It further adds, "Nay, God raised him up unto

himself, and God is exalted in Power, wise" (Surah 4:158).'

'So, your interpretation is that the Qur'an is only denying that the Jews killed him', Atif interrupted.

His mother was by now becoming a little impatient and advised him to be quiet and to let me finish. Atif apologised and said, 'Sorry, brother! Go on, please.'

I carried on, 'Most of the Muslim commentators, *Mufassirin*, of the Qur'an believe that the Jews failed in their treacherous plot to kill Jesus. They claim that the Roman soldiers arrested a person who had a striking resemblance to Jesus, while Jesus himself was lifted alive to Heaven.

'They all seem to accept a crucifixion as an historical fact but deny that it was Jesus who was actually crucified. God made someone else look just like Jesus, yet it appeared to the Jews that they had crucified Jesus himself. Muslim commentators have different names on their list. Some say Judas Iscariot was slain in Jesus' place; others say Simon of Cyrene. Some name him as Sergus while others call him Tityanus, Titabus or Titanus. Whoever it was, if God made his face to look like that of Jesus at that moment so people were 'taken in', would this not be an intolerable deception? How could Jesus, the prophet of God, allow such a terrible deception?

'If God wanted to raise Jesus to heaven, why was it necessary to victimise a bystander? If we believe that it was someone else on the cross and God made his face look like that of Jesus to mislead people, this would mean that God is one who deceives and such a notion is intolerable. Such a theory engages God in a cheap deceptive charade. I believe that the whole incident should be understood in the light of the narratives as recorded in the Bible, that Christ indeed was crucified; he did die and on the third day he rose again. After having fellowship with his disciples for forty days he ascended into heaven in their sight.'

I paused and waited for their reaction. They both were in deep thought. Atif's mother at last looked at me and said, 'I have often wondered, would God allow one who is described in the Qur'an as being eminent in this world and in the next to be murdered by those who were not honouring God?'

I certainly agreed with her and added, 'If there was anyone in history who did not deserve to be killed, it was Jesus. However, the Bible puts it differently. Its view is: Christ died; he was buried and on the third day he rose, thereby gaining victory over death. Let us not separate his crucifixion and death from his victorious resurrection. Though God allowed him to die, he did not let death consume him eternally. He rose to life victoriously as he himself has said: "I am the Living One; I was dead, and behold I am alive for ever and ever!" (Revelation 1:18).'

We could not continue the discussion because a friend of hers arrived unexpectedly, and was practising *pardah*, the veil. So Atif and I went into the adjacent room and continued our discussion. He was surprised when I mentioned that although only one verse in the Qur'an said that the Jews did not kill or crucify Jesus, there were other references which suggested that he did die. Qur'anic references (Surah 19:33; 3:55 and 5:117) when looked at in context deal with a similar subject (for example 2:240 and 6:60), so one can say clearly that it is God who was to be the ultimate cause of his death rather than any person or persons.

I told Atif that Jesus once said to his followers, 'Do not be afraid of those who kill the body but cannot kill the soul. Rather be afraid of the One who can destroy both soul and body in hell' (Matthew 10:28). If the soul of an ordinary being cannot be killed by mortals, how could the Jews ever say that they crucified and killed the *'word'* and the *'spirit'* of God. The biblical explanation of the whole matter is more acceptable than all other interpretations.

I did not know how many of the things I said had convinced Atif. That was my last meeting with him.

The Bible was still open at the passage I had read earlier. I put the Bible on the table but, after a while in prayer, my mind was still thinking about Atif, about his loving mother. I also thought of those I had met in past years. Though some rejected, there were others who understood the message of assurance as presented by Jesus, but they were reluctant to follow.

'What would people say?' was usually their worry. Whether right or wrong, since Islam was the faith of their fathers, their families and their community, they felt obliged to follow in the same faith. Some argued that perhaps God himself did not want them to follow only one path. 'If God wanted us to follow his only way', they argued, 'he would have compelled us to do so.'

Some would hide behind a Qur'anic passage which suggests that if God had wanted he would have made all human beings into one community (Surah 5:48).

This used to open the doors to whether the passage is about groups of people of colour, languages and habits, or whether God was really talking about telling one people to follow one way and the other group of people to follow another way. He is not a God of confusion nor he is capricious.

That night in my prayer, I remembered them all. When I finished praying and opened my eyes, it was pitch dark. The electricity had gone off. By touch, I found my way to the kitchen and found a candle. I went out into the street to see what had happened and soon found that a transformer a block away had been on fire and was still smouldering. Such things happen in Karachi. For several months, the air is filled with sea salt, which leaves a salty layer on the surface of such old transformers, so when rain comes, it acts like a conductor and causes power failure.

Someone shouted in the dark, 'Get this *Chohra* out so that there may be some light.' Hearing this I quietly closed the door, changed my clothes and went to bed. Though I was tired, sleep was something far from me. 'Why, Lord, why can people be so sarcastic and vicious?'

12

More Than Conquerors

Early in the morning there was a knock on the door. I
got up to see who it was. It was unusual to see the postman at the door with a registered letter. Not having a
permanent address, I usually gave my work address
for correspondence. I signed to receive it. First I
thought it was from the university but soon realised
that it was from the postal services where I worked.
The postman left but I remained standing at the door
and quickly opened it. I could not believe it. The sub-
committee had decided to terminate my services. It
took me a few minutes to overcome the shock. With a
heavy heart I closed the door. For a while I could not
take it in. It seemed like the end of another era.

I decided to go to the office and submit an appeal.
According to the employees' handbook, I should have
had a hearing but in some countries, clauses and codes
are made to adorn pages of manuals only. An hour
later I was standing at the bus stop. My landlord was
also going somewhere. Just before his bus arrived, he
told me that due to some unavoidable circumstances I
would have to find somewhere else to live. Here was
another shock of the day. Finding a place to live is not
as easy as going to a hotel and hiring a room.

The bus arrived. I was fortunate to find some room on the footboard to stand. After a few stops, I was able to move inside the crowded bus. Through the window I saw a few cars and taxis with only one or two passengers and sighed, 'Wouldn't it be nice if people travelling with empty seats gave lifts to others?'

The passenger next to me looked at me. I thought perhaps he was thinking that I was out of my mind or a runaway from a mental hospital. On the other hand, he may not have thought anything at all and it was just me being suspicious.

At the office I waited and waited as usual. No one in authority was willing to see me there. I tried to make an appointment but was refused. I was about to fill an application form for an appointment when the Superintendent came to the door and called me in. I sighed with relief. He asked the porter for some cold drinks and asked me to occupy one of the chairs next to his big desk.

The phone rang. He quickly picked it up as he was waiting for it. He was so joyful in his conversation. Cold drinks arrived, one for him and one for me. It was the same room where a couple of years before I came with a reference from his friend and so he made sure that I had the job.

While still on the phone he made a sign to me to have my cold drink. After finishing his conversation, he himself made another call, talking about some party that night he was having at his house. After retiring from a lengthy detail of 'do's and don'ts' on the phone, he asked me for the purpose of seeing him. I showed him the termination letter with his signature on it. Seeing the letter, he laughed.

'Oh, this. Forget it. You can rejoin, if you want to.' He looked hopeful. 'There is one condition.' He paused. It seemed like an eternity.

'You will not go round and tell people about your belief.'

'Sir, I do not impose my faith on anybody. However, when I am asked, I do respond by sharing with them during the tea or lunch breaks', I apologised.

'Religion is not going to feed you. Just tell them you are not a Christian any more though in your heart you may be', he advised me. 'No one would care whether you recite your prayers or not. There are many Muslims who for their whole life may not see the face of a mosque and yet claim to be Muslims. Look, Masood, I myself do not perform all the prayers. For your sake, for your job, for the sake of your friends and your parents can't you make just this adjustment?'

'Sir, my suspension and termination was not because of my faith but because of allegations of negligence and other irregularities. So why is my faith being brought into question now?'

He looked at my file and said, 'That is true. I know all those allegations are just not right, but you know that I have a boss who would like his nephew to take your place. And you know what ... he is a staunch Muslim. Since he came to know about your apostasy, he has been pestering me to find ways to get rid of you. However, if you just renounce what you do, I will make sure that no harm comes to you. After all, you are a hard-working and honest man and I don't want to see you end like Atif.' After a silent pause he said, 'He was questioning a lot and see what happened to him.'

'But Sir, it is not even Islamic to live like a hypocrite. I cannot do that.' Before I could continue the phone rang and he said, 'I have many things to do. Go home. Think about it and come back tomorrow.' He waved his hand to say goodbye and picked up the phone.

I left his office. A colleague at the accounts office saw me and asked me if I could join him for a cup of tea. I allowed myself to go. He enquired about the conversation that took place between me and the head in the office, but I declined to reveal it to him. He was still kind, and he gave me my remaining salary and wished me good luck in finding a new job and a place to live.

It was the fortieth day since Atif had left this world. His relatives had organised a religious ritual known as *chehulum*. His brother, Hassan, had reluctantly invited me and I was not sure whether to go or not. I bought a few garlands and roses wrapped in a damp newspaper to keep them fresh. The florist was so kind as to put them in a nice big brown bag.

It took another two hours to reach the cemetery. Unusually, there were several people in the graveyard. For some people, Thursday afternoon is a special time. Some would visit the graves of saintly people for blessings. However, I was here not for that kind of blessing but just to identify myself as having a friend who was special. After laying the flowers at his grave, I sat by the side of it. A marble stone slab had been erected by his family with the inscription of his name 'Atif Zafar Mahmood', and the dates of his birth and death. To embellish graves with big tombstones or to elaborate the structure is forbidden in Islam. Still, such graves are a common sight on Muslim graveyards. I looked around. There were some graves simply covered with earth, heaped up in semicircular or roof-shaped forms.

Yet I could also see others that looked as if a mauso-leum had been built over the graves. Still others had a lamp holder at the head of the tomb on which candles are burnt or oil lamps lit on Thursday evenings. There were a few graves which had a boundary around them, and with a marble stone slab on which the name and dates of birth and death of the deceased were written along with Qur'anic verse or poetry.

I looked at the slab and there, along with his name, date of birth and death was inscribed a couplet in the Urdu language which caught my attention more than anything:

Kaya Khulay jo kabi neh tha penha,
Kaya milay jo kabi juda neh huwa.
(You found Him you think, Who never did hide? And met Him who ever was by thy side?)

I had seen this verse in stylish calligraphy on one of the wall in Atif's room. I remembered him saying, 'Masood! You may think you have found God but was he ever lost? He is always there beside you. It is just that you have somehow recognised his presence around you.'

I could sense the Sufi mysticism but could not ignore the reality of his comments. Sitting there, tears flowed from my eyes. I just could not bear it.

'Don't you hate it when people cry over living peo-ple?' I looked up. A very old man just passed me hold-ing a young boy's hand. Before I could say or ask anything, I saw Hassan along with a group of people coming towards the grave. I stood aside and said greet-ings to him and others. Flowers were laid. The atmo-sphere was full of the smell of roses and scent. Visiting

graves is not a common practice but most people visit
the graves of their relatives during the first month of
their burial and then on special occasions to lay flowers
and recite some prayers.

After a little spray of water from a can, the *Moulvi
Sahib* who came with them raised his hands in prayer.
Prayers (*Dua*) for the dead are not universal in Islam. In
such prayers the first chapter of the Qur'an known as
the *fatiha* is recited. After the *fatiha* everyone started to
leave, so I followed. At the gate I stood in reverence
until Hassan and those who came with him left. 'Are
you not going to their home?' someone asked me. 'Yes,
I am.'

'I can give you a lift.' He revved his motor cycle. I
thanked him for his offer and sat behind him. After half
an hour we were at Atif's home. According to custom,
we removed our shoes at the door of the sitting room
and joined others sitting on the white sheet that had
been laid from wall to wall on the floor.

The ritual of *Chihlam* concludes the time of mourning. Prayers are said and a meal is served to those in
attendance and to the poor on the street. The prayers
usually consist of Qur'anic recitations offered for the
benefit of the deceased person so that his sins may be
forgiven. The ceremony of the recitation on such occasions is called *qul*, because it consists of reciting the
chapters of the Qur'an which begin with the word *qul*
(Surah 109, 112, 113 and 114).

Though in body I was there in the room with the
mourners, my mind was far away, thinking of how
time passed. Forty days ago Atif was living, walking
and talking, but now he was not there. The words of
the prayer at his funeral were still afresh in my mind:

O Allah forgive our alive and dead, our present and absent, our young and old, and our males and females. O Allah to whom you give life let him live in the observation of Islam (surrender to God) and to whom you give death let him die in the state of having full faith.

Although I was sitting there quietly like others, I just could not stop asking myself if it was valid to pray for the deceased so that God could intercede and accept that person into his paradise. Is it necessary for the person to have repented before his death? Will there be remission at last for those who reject God and his plan for people? The only answer I could come to was to worry about the living not about those who have finished their duration of life on this earth.

The only response I could think of was, 'Leave that to God and be available to those who still have a breath of life in them; those who still have a chance, go and tell them to believe in the assurance provided by God himself. It is not because of our good deeds but because, as God's creation, he has offered it to us.'

I remembered one of Atif's friends who, after a lengthy discussion, had asked me if after my death the angel of God asked me what my religion was, what I would say.

'Islam', I abruptly replied.

It did not surprise Atif but his friend looked at me mouth open wide, 'How come? Are you not a Christian?'

'Yes I am, but more than that I am a Muslim and Islam is my way of life.'

I had to explain to him that the word Muslim itself is interpreted by Muslims as 'one who has surrendered himself to God' and Islam means 'to surrender to (God), to make peace with (God)'. I believe that by believing in Christ and by obeying what Jesus has commanded, I have surrendered myself to God, thus I am a Muslim and my *din*, faith, is Islam.

There were still people coming to attend the occasion. Amongst the late arrivals was also my supervisor. He came straight towards me saying, *'Esai Ba'bay! Kiya hal hai?'* (Christian baby! How are you?)

I just replied, *'Alhamdu lilah!'* (All praises to God) and made some room for him. He very well knew that Atif was my best friend but never liked our having religious conversations. He himself was a staunch Muslim who tried to fulfil all commands of following the ritual law and yet one could see lot of pitfalls in his daily working in the office.

'Friend! Why don't you leave this family alone. You knew Atif. He is no more. Just go your way. You Christians, wherever you go you bring problems to other peoples' family life.' He raised his voice deliberately so that others could hear him.

'Sir, please, this is not the place and time', I begged him.

'What do you mean, you apostate, infidel?' He stood up enraged and looked towards Hassan sitting in a corner on the other side of the room and complained to him, 'Brother Hassan! You should not have allowed this wretched man to come in.'

Then he addressed all in the room, 'Brothers! This is an apostate. He does not believe in Muhammad and yet loves to sit among those who believe in Him. While you send blessing on him, he keeps saying, "God forbid." '

I did not know what to do. I just stood and said, 'It is true that I am a believer in Christ but this is a clear lie that while you bless the name of the prophet of Islam, I keep saying, "God forbid". It was in the teaching of the Prophet of Islam and his holy Qur'an that I first found out about Christ. However, this is not the time and place to go into this detail. Maybe some other time. May the Lord's blessing be with you all.'

I quickly realised that to stay there was not right and walked out of the room. Putting my shoes on I could hear a murmur in the room. Hassan with another person caught up with me at the main gate of the house. They apologised for the manner in which my supervisor had spoken. I told them that I was not leaving because of any hurt to me but because my presence might be a stumbling block and cause grievance to Hassan and his family and his friends. Hassan and his friends agreed that it was best that I should leave. We shook hands and I left.

All the way home, I kept thinking about what had happened earlier and I also felt pity. Still, there were other things on my mind. The order of priorities had to be considered. Is it getting a job? Is it accommodation? I was not able to think straight. When I reached home, I was glad to find that the electricity had been restored. After a quick wash and brush up, I ate the take-away I had bought at the bus stop in the city.

After washing up in the kitchen and as I was about to make some tea, my landlord called on me. We sat for a while. He explained how neighbours in the vicinity were upset that he rented his house to me, since I was an infidel and an apostate. He returned to me the money he held as deposit for the next three months' rent, and pleaded with me to vacate the house in the next few days. He was more concerned about the Imam of the mosque who had excited neighbours by saying that, as an apostate, I was worthy of capital punishment. I did not know what to say, whether to thank him for the information or to plead with him to let me live there until I had found some place to move to.

When he left, I just went on my knees and pleaded with God not to leave me alone. I complained, asking why he was not helping me. When I could no longer bear the pain in my knees because of the hard cement of the floor, I got up and walked around in the courtyard. In such situations the Scriptures have always comforted me, so I decided to read. I went into the room, got the Bible and started reading. There it was, a passage dealing with my situation:

And we know that in all things God works for the good of those who love him, who have been called according to his purpose... What, then, shall we say in response to this? If God is for us, who can be against us? He who did not spare his own Son, but gave him up for us all – how will he not also, along with him, graciously give us all things? Who will bring any charge against those whom God has chosen? It is God who justifies. Who is he that condemns? Christ Jesus, who died – more than that, who was raised to life – is at the right hand of God and is also interceding for us. Who shall separate us from the love of Christ? Shall trouble or hardship or persecution or famine or nakedness or danger or sword? ... No, in all these things we are more than conquerors through him who loved us. For I am convinced that neither death nor life, neither angels nor demons, neither the present nor the future, nor anything else in all creation, will be able to separate us from the love of God that is in Christ Jesus our Lord (Romans 8:28,31–39).

I thanked God for this consolation. Sometime later, when I was trying to have some sleep, I seemed to have been asking why some Muslims celebrate the rituals of *Soium*, and *Chehlum*. Somehow I thought about Christ's resurrection on the third day and his ascension forty days later. With such thoughts I finally went to sleep.

When I woke up, it was morning. It was Sunday so I decided to attend the church in the city and later start job hunting. I hurried in order to be on time and, two hours later, I was with the congregation among whom I knew a few friends including my elderly friend Mr Massey. As usual the fellowship and worship was heart warming.

After meeting several friends, I was about to set off to start with my other quests when a gentleman by the name of Nasim shook hands with me. This was the second time we had met. Previously, we had met when he wanted to help one of his Muslim friends to know more about faith in Jesus, so I gladly shared with his friends my testimony of how I accepted Christ. Nasim invited me to a quick cup of tea which I could not refuse.

During our discussion, he came to know that I was looking for a job and he mentioned that there was a clerical post vacant at the hospital where he worked. As he was about to go back to resume his duty that afternoon, I went along with him to the hospital. He introduced me to the director and left me with him. I had my qualifications and other papers with me; seeing all the papers, and after some searching questions, he gave me a form to fill in. He led me to a hall where I could sit and write. Ten minutes later I was at his door again. He called me in, and after an interview with him and the administrator also present, I was again asked to wait outside in the hall for a while.

Half an hour later, the director invited me in his office and to my surprise he offered me the job on probation for six months. The very next day I started and a few days later when the director came to know that I was also searching for accommodation, he was persuasive enough to convince the housing department to allocate me a room with another bachelor living in one of the hospital's flats.

What more could I have asked for? New job, new people, more friends. However, I did not forget my old friends and colleagues and even those who were upset with me. Still when I remember them, I pray for them.

And I do not fail to remember Atif, his friendship, and his thirst to know about Jesus.

My university application failed that year, and the following year, for a variety of reasons. But that is another story. Suffice to say, the Lord eventually brought me to Britain to complete my studies and proved a means of sharing Christ's love with nearly two million Muslims.

Meanwhile, back in Karachi, a year after moving into

my new flat, I was rearranging my library. Atif's copy of the Bible, the one that his brother had returned to me fell on the floor. I quickly picked it up. It was open at a page towards the end of the gospel according to Luke where a discourse between Jesus and two other people who were crucified along with him is mentioned. I read the two verses Atif had underlined:

> 'Jesus, remember me when you come into your kingdom.' Jesus answered him, 'I tell you the truth, today you will be with me in paradise' (Luke 23:42–43).

On the margin Atif had scribbled:

> O, Master of the universe, Jesus, the unique! Let your glance of mercy be on me too. I am not worthy to ask for a place in your paradise. Grant me, a wretched sinner, if at all possible, to be the doormat of the door of your paradise through which your companions will come and go.